100 QUICK ESSAYS

From
@TheDevoutHumorist

KYLE WOODRUFF

For those waking up.

Dear Reader,

What you have here is a collection of random ideas expressed within the 2,200-character limit of Instagram. They're organized in no particular order and by no means need to be read that way. The best approach to reading this book could be flipping to a random page and beginning there, or perhaps perusing the Table of Contents and picking a title that stands out at the time of doing so.

These essays are loosely categorized by subject—such as childhood inspirations, float tank meditations, or societal observations—and even more loosely organized by a timeline from youth to the present, so, if you choose to read them in order, just know that's what you're in for.

These stories were also written as bite-sized reflections, so I believe they're meant to be consumed the same way. What I mean is that this book wasn't designed to be a page-turner, but rather a collection of one-off meditations. It's more like a coffee table book, a bedside read, or—dare I say—for the toilet bowl (if you're into that sort of thing).

Happy pooping,
The Author

CONTENTS

PIN THE TAIL 1
SHREDDER 3
EARLY BETRAYAL 5
MR. CREEPY 7
NO INNER CHILD LEFT BEHIND 9
ME AND SOME CHILDREN 11
FRUITS AND FLOWERS 13
PRESERVING THE YOUTH 15
KICKBALL 17
CHICKEN BOOTH 19
FAMILY GAME NIGHT 21
STINKY ROOMMATES 23
GROWING UP 25
ARCHERY LESSONS 27
PIGEON WENCH 29
EGYPTIAN NUISANCE 31
CONTEMPORARY "ART" MUSEUM 33
MOUNT TRASHMORE 35
ICE MAKER OBVIOUSNESS 37
IGUANA SNIPER 39
UBER DRIVER MADNESS 41
PROCREATION LIMITATION 43
HAMBURGERS & BUREACRACY 45
BOO-BOO-RU 47
ACIDIC ILLUSIONS 49
PLAY THE GAME 51
WAR PAINT 53

PLANTAR FASCIITIS	55
PLANTAR FASCIITIS 2	57
DON'T BE AN ALBATROSS	59
LITTER BUGS	61
YA KNOW?	63
SURFING AT SUNRISE	65
THOUGHTLESS BASTARDS 1	67
THOUGHTLESS BASTARDS 2	69
DOCILITY	71
YOU FREAK!	73
"WHY DO WE EVEN HAVE MOTHERS!?"	75
"THIS ALWAYS HAPPENS TO ME!"	77
JAWS	79
STROLLER DADDY	81
HOMELESS GAL	83
BEACH PHILOSOPHER	85
PSYCHO	87
PULL-UPS AT CHURCH	89
SHUT UP AND LISTEN	91
HELP	93
SELFISHLY SERVING OTHERS?	95
UNRESOLVING CONFLICT	97
WINNING AN OSCAR	99
PING PONG RESENTMENT	101
DEFLECTING PRAISE	103
ARGUMENTS ARE A MIRROR	105
FLIGHT PRAYERS	107
FLOWING TO THE DENTIST	109
LET GO OF THE STEERING WHEEL	111
JEFFREY DAHMER 1	113
JEFFREY DAHMER 2	115

THE UNABOMBER	117
WESTERN NOSTALGIA	119
ARE YOU DEAD INSIDE?	121
LEWIS & CLARK	123
HAKUNA MATATA	125
GARDEN PARALLEL	127
HORSE-AND-BUGGY	129
RELIGIOUS BAGGAGE	131
SOME THINGS SHOULD NEVER CHANGE	133
DONKEY > MARY	135
BELL CURVE	137
APHRODITE	139
MAD MINUTE	141
GHOSTS OF THE PAST	143
FOR ARGUMENT'S SAKE	145
PRODUCTIVITY IS THE DEVIL	147
WHERE'S THE OFF SWITCH?	149
NEITZSCHE FOR MORONS	151
SMOOTH RIDER	153
AREN'T I THOUGH?	155
BE THE GARDNER	157
NOTES FROM FLOATS	159
THIRTY YEARS IN THREE HOURS	161
NIRVANA	163
PIZZA OR BUST	165
GETTING HUMBLED	167
SMILE IN THE FACE OF _____.	169
BUDWEISER & CAT PISS	171
LETTING GO OF CONTROL	173
THE KEY?	175
DROP IT LIKE IT'S HOT	177

G.I. JOE	179
"ALWAYS TAKE BODY PARTS WITH YOU."	181
TRUE BRAVERY	183
STRANGER STRANGLER	185
CHAOS OR FATE?	187
PYRAMID OF PRIORITIZATION	189
DHARMA BUMS	191
LIKE LIGHTNING	193
DEATH GRIP	195
NOSTALGIA	197
THE BUTTERFLY LADY	199

PIN THE TAIL

*Do not mix truth with falsehood or
hide the truth knowingly.*
—The Qur'an 2:42

One of my earliest memories is of lying. (How's that for entering consciousness?) I'm not proud of it, which is probably why it stuck so hard, but I thought cheating was the way to get ahead back then.

To set the scene, my extended family was on vacation—which I deemed a "beach-cation," due to my youthfully ignorant grasp of words and an acute observation of where this detour from normal life took place.

During rainy days on beach-cation (which I recall feeling were a divine injustice), we'd play indoor games for entertainment. These included your stereotypical board and card games, of course, but sometimes the adults would teach us new games, like Pin The Tail On The Donkey.

This was no ordinary game of Pin The Tail On The Donkey, however; there were stakes. Arcade tokens for the winner, to be exact: entertainment currency for the local coin-operated game center we'd be attending during this annual visit.

Now, I sat back and observed a few foolish-looking cousins bumping into walls after being spun around or wandering into donkey-less rooms while blind, and I was determined not to be a loser like them. Fortunately, when it came time to blindfold me, my uncle did a poor job with the bandana, and there was a crack at the bottom through which I could kinda, sorta, maybe see.

Without knowing how to make myself look convincingly lucky, I waltzed right up to the poster and pinned the tail where any anatomically correct donkey had one.

"Could you see?" my uncle said.

"No!" I said.

"Tell the truth," he said.

"I swear!" I said.

And—bless his heart—he pried no further and coughed up the coin.

But I remember holding those tokens in my hand, feeling something I'm not even sure I could have named back then: guilt.

I didn't earn those coins, not honestly anyway. I lied, and that didn't feel good, and I never wanted to feel that again.

Consider this my public admission that I, the dishonest donkey-pinner, did wrong. I hope this confession absolves me of my sin and frees me from the guilt I've been holding onto all these years.

Sorry, Uncle T!

SHREDDER

Like the child, innocently making thousands of mistakes,
his father teaches him, and scolds him so many times,
but still, he hugs him close in his embrace.
Please forgive my past actions, God,
and place me on Your path for the future.
   —Siri Guru Granth - Ang 624

When I turned seven, I had some "friends" over for a birthday party. I put "friends" in quotations because one of those backstabbing munchkins smeared the term with their appalling behavior that day.

One of my pals gifted me the most prized Ninja Turtles action figures on the market at the time, revealed for all to see during the post-cake unwrapping ceremony. But it was a short-lived affair between that toy and me because by the time the party was over and all my friends were gone, so too was Shredder—the main villain of the Ninja Turtles franchise. (I see the irony now, with the evil character being stolen. Like does attract like, it seems!)

Which of these two-faced companions felt so impoverished financially and morally that they had the audacity to ruin the celebration of *my* birth?

Was it Todd, you ask? The spoiled only child whose love for toys outweighed his love for his friend? Or Jerry? Putting on a friendly facade since kindergarten while plotting this day? Or perhaps Mark, the very gifter of the toy himself, who couldn't bear to part with such awesomeness, so he snatched it, fueled by jealous rage.

This early instance of betrayal may seem silly now, but to the seven-year-old boy whose love for toys shaped his faith in humanity, who knows what kind of imprint this had? Did it impart the notion that even your closest friends can't be trusted? Were birthday celebrations entwined with feelings of betrayal? Who knows how deep the Ninja Turtle scandal goes?

Did my "friend" ever learn that that's no way to get ahead in life? Did they walk away carrying the burden of guilt in their pocket along with my new toy?

Or did that same steal-to-get-ahead mentality follow them in the future, manifesting itself in adult ways?

Are they still holding onto Shredder, like a family heirloom—*my* family heirloom—to be passed on to *their* son, along with whatever generational shame plagues such family lines?

Where does it stop? When does the madness end?

Whoever it was, if you fess up now, *maybe* I'll forgive you. But do it before it's too late, before the scorching flames of Hell engulf your toy-stealing soul.

EARLY BETRAYAL

*Whenever you speak, speak justly,
even if a near relative is concerned.*
—The Qur'an 6:152

I went into a recent meditation with the intention of reflecting on why I can be such a cold jerk at times. What emerged from the depths of the oddball memory banks was something I hadn't thought about in years. I was standing on the edge of a boat launch with a cousin of mine, whom I didn't get to see very often. We had just returned from a fishing trip with my dad, and he and I were playing on the shore.

My cousin was older and cooler, someone I looked up to, so I was shocked when I did something apparently foolish, and he immediately told on me. This resulted not only in my father scolding me, but I even got put in timeout when we got home.

Now, from your perspective, looking onto someone else's childhood, I'm sure this seems like no big deal. "So you had to sit in timeout for a few minutes," the critic says. "There are children starving in China!" But looking back through the eyes of a child who had little to no life experience for comparison, what happened here was an early act of betrayal by someone I admired.

To be thrown under the bus like that, and for seemingly no reason at all? Not to mention the fact that you come into *my* house, get *me* put in timeout, and then spend 1-on-1 time with *my* dad? Well, that didn't sit right with me at all.

You better believe I stewed in that comfy prison chair while building a deep hatred for tattletales. And the smug look on his face while I was sentenced to twenty minutes of incarceration was the most punchable face I've seen to this day. It brewed a resentment in me that I'd apparently held onto for the next two decades.

That is until I finally let it go.

MR. CREEPY

The Master said,
"The firm, the enduring, the simple, and the modest
are near to virtue."
—Analects of Confucius - Book 13, Chapter 27

In elementary school, I had a music teacher named Mr. Creepy, or something like that. I remember thinning wisps of gray, wrinkled skin over a bony frame, and disturbingly yellow fingernails, grown out for the purpose of plucking guitar strings. I didn't have much life experience then, but I knew he was strange from the moment I saw him.

One day, Mr. Creepy brought in an old-school projector, the kind that rattled as it shifted from one slide to the next, and he gave us an unsolicited glimpse into one of his personal endeavors. We put aside aimlessly blowing into our recorders for a day to listen to the story of an adventure he'd been on. I don't recall the specific details of where, when, or why, but he shuffled through slides of a sabbatical that, in retrospect, seemed like a spiritual journey.

In short, he had abandoned all his worldly possessions for thirty days (including his shirt, if my memory serves me) and went off to live in the woods. I mean *really* live in the woods. This guy carved his own canoe out of a tree and paddled up a river, for Pete's sake. This was no weekend camping trip with a propane stove; he was out there.

At that age, I had no interest in Mr. Creepy or his personal affairs (nor the recorder, for that matter), but the older I get, the more there's a nagging feeling that tugs at my sleeve, urging me to return to a simpler lifestyle. It's an itch you can't scratch with a rotisserie chicken from Costco, and I wish I could have appreciated what Mr. Creepy was trying to share back then.

This world of office jobs and technology: it's so... so...

Rush hours and coffee pots and thirty-minute lunch breaks: Is this what we're here for? As much as I enjoy shoveling down a store-bought meal in a climate-controlled room, part of me longs to be like Mr. Creepy on sabbatical. The prospect of survival breathing down your neck, the feeling of elation after catching your own meal, the connectivity with the world around you: these are the kinds of things that make you feel *alive*, or so I assume.

Mr. Creepy was old and decrepit back then, so I'd be shocked if he were still around to read this now, but if you're out there, Creeps, just know that I finally appreciate what you were trying to inspire.

NO INNER CHILD LEFT BEHIND

Folly is bound up in the heart of a child,
but the rod of discipline will drive it far away.
—*Proverbs 22:15*

"It's too early in the morning for AC/DC!" my father yelled over his nephew's poor choice of song. Playful scolds like these were often dished out during long car rides with rambunctious teens.

He was right, of course, being 6 a.m. and all. The only reason to play that kind of music at that kind of volume at that kind of hour was just to get a rise out of the old man.

These are the memories etched in my brain from youth: the silly, the nonsensical, the borderline insane. Today, I'm more likely to be the one dialing down the AC/DC and leaning toward the brink of sanity.

In the recess age of life, I can recall seeing a playground and running rampant through hunks of metal for hours without getting bored. Yesterday, I strolled by a playground and didn't even look twice. All I can see now is the fruitless cycle of fleeting thrills that exceeds the cost-benefit ratio in the labor-to-fun department.

Could I even find entertainment in the simple thrills of a swing set anymore? Or has the overwhelming sense of existential crisis choked out any hopes for childhood pleasure?

Where does that innate sense of silliness go, I wonder? When do these traits get buried under responsibilities and bills?

Is this why people drink and indulge in substances? To temporarily poison their sense of adulthood in order to tap into their inner child?

Somewhere behind the gates of inhibition lives that long-lost sense of childhood wonder, itching for an excuse to break out again.

The question is: Can you still access that part of yourself without inebriation?

Yesterday at the gym, my friend and I were messing with some teenager by spewing the most absurd rhetoric of nonsensical gobbledygook that spun this poor child's head around. The snickering laughter that resulted from this verbal abuse brought a degree of boyhood boisterousness bubbling back to the surface. This flash of adolescent nonsense was a sign that hope still exists, and excessive humor may just be the key to unlocking those gates in sobriety.

Vote for me in this coming election, and I'll enact a "No Inner Child Left Behind" campaign.

ME AND SOME CHILDREN

Just realize where you come from:
This is the essence of wisdom.
—Tao Te Ching - Verse 14

I was hanging out with some children yesterday. (Well, it wasn't just me and some children; that'd be weird. It was a Thanksgiving gathering, mind you.) The point is, I couldn't help but notice the level of joy that exists in kids around the age of five. Pure giggling, non-stop, over the most insignificant things. I can't remember the last time I experienced that much joy over seemingly nothing. I can't even recall the last time I experienced that much joy over *something*, regardless of the amount of sugar I've consumed.

At what age does that stop, I wonder? When does life squeeze it out of us with trauma, bills, and responsibilities? Is it psychological, where life experience puts things in perspective? Or is it chemical, where aging doesn't trigger the same dopamine release in our brains? Are the years we barely remember really the most joy-filled years of our lives?

It seems sad, but then again, life might be strange if spinning around the floor and screaming in ecstasy over games of tag tickled us the same way as adults as it did when we were children. Not to mention the tears that come moments later when repeating chants of "I want a lollipop!" yield no reward.

Perhaps we just have to cherish whatever little sparks of joy come our way as we grow older. Excuse me while I gorge myself on leftovers and watch World Cup goals being scored.

FRUITS AND FLOWERS

The Master said,
"There are shoots that never come to flower,
and there are flowers that never bear fruit."
—Analects of Confucius - Book 9, Chapter 22

How does this play out long term? I wondered this as I observed three girls and a boy playing under the half-assed supervision of one of their fathers, who was preoccupied with fishing.

Here's what happened:

- Girl A threw seaweed at the boy, and the boy started crying.
- Girl A ran away to play with girl B, pretending like she had nothing to do with the tears.
- The boy ran to his father, and while being half-ass comforted, girl C shared her toy with the boy, and the tears immediately vanished.

What kind of stories and habits were being reinforced for the long haul here?

For example:
- Girl A learns that she can escape responsibility if she runs away from things that might get her in trouble.
- The boy learns that if he cries over little things, others will give him stuff to make him feel better.
- Girl C learns that if she gives things to people who are upset, they'll like her.

I fear that fatherhood, if it's ever in the cards, may one day short-circuit my over-analytical brain. All I could wonder was, *Will these shoots come to flower? Or will they wither on the vine before they bear fruit?* (I guess in this metaphor, they're toxic flowers or poison berries, but perhaps I'm stretching here.)

Anyway, can you think of any patterns like this that you may have learned back when the memories are a bit fuzzy?

PRESERVING THE YOUTH

The beauty of youth and flowers are guests for only a few days.
Like the leaves of the water-lily,
they wither and fade and finally die.
Be happy, dear beloved,
as long as your youth is fresh and delightful.
But your days are few—
you have grown weary, and now your body has grown old.
—Siri Guru Granth - Ang 23

When I lived in California, I met this guy who preached a philosophy of "preserving the youth." When I asked what he meant, he told me to meet him at a nearby park the next day.

In the parking lot, he handed me a small and brightly colored net before marching up a flight of stairs holding a jar. I didn't even ask what it was for, just followed him halfway up until something caught his eye.

"Stand right there," he said, hovering over a tightly-knit shrub next to the stairs. I stood stair-side of him, staring questioningly, when all of a sudden, he began shaking the back side of the shrub. Right then, a small lizard shot out across the stairs past my feet as he yelled, "Get him!"

Too little, too late, I swiped the net at the scampering reptile, and it was gone into a bush on the other side. "You're gonna have to be quicker than that," said Lizard Man, marching up the stairs.

Again, something caught his eye, and he lined up outside another bush.

Shake, shake, shake.

Pyooom!

Swat.

Miss.

I couldn't help but laugh at my own second failure.

"Come on," said Lizard Man, "you're makin' us look bad!"

"Alright, alright," I laughed. "I've got the next one."

And I did. And another, and another, before we ran out of stair bushes to shake.

From there, we took our bounty back to his house, where we ate them.

(Just kidding. We didn't eat park lizards.)

…where we put them in a tank and caught some bugs for them to eat, ordering a pizza for ourselves as we watched.

After an hour, we let them go, watching them scurry off to new bushes some insurmountable distance away for a lizard to ever get home. Hopefully they didn't have families.

Anyway, the experience was such a simple way to tap into that long-lost inner child who gets too neglected in the face of adulthood. And, honestly, just a refreshing way to spend an afternoon.

So I ask you, dear reader: What are you doing to preserve the youth today?

KICKBALL

Winning gives birth to hostility.
Losing, one lies down in pain.
The calmed lie down with ease,
having set winning and losing aside.
—The Dhammapada - Chapter 15, Verse 201

I played kickball last weekend, for the first time since fifth grade. A bunch of middle-aged guys and gals from the gym organized the game in a local park. It was hilarious to watch.

I used to play soccer [brushes off shoulder], so I was alright in the kicking department, but some of my peers were, well, less athletically inclined. Coordination below the waist is lacking for most people who have never played sports requiring coordination below the waist, and observing a sudden late-life need for this skill in others is just darn fun.

One guy whiffed at a slow roller so hard you thought he might be Charlie Brown.

"I'm not wearing my glasses!" he belted out. Sure, sure, sure.

People with no inkling of baseball-like rules were the best, slicing a kick over the fence along the foul line and arguing for a home run and whatnot. Good times. Good times.

The best part was how quickly the competitive fifth-grade nature snaps back when the game is on the line going into the last inning, arguing over close calls the way you would at recess, half-seriously accusing people you hardly know of being cheaters in a nonsense sport that would leave you sore enough to remember how old you are. There's something magical about the way old gym class games turn grown-ups into kids again.

Ahh, Life: Why do you bury these joyful moments under so many responsibilities? Why do decades pass between matches on the kickball fields of existence?

Don't get it confused: Despite the above Buddhist "wisdom," there are winners and losers in this life. Clearly, Buddha never kicked the winning RBI in an elementary school battle in the bottom of the ninth. In fact, the more I think about it, the more I realize this was probably written by someone picked last in gym class every time. Loser.

Now, if you have the balls to find out which one you are, clear your schedule for Sunday. Round two is on.

CHICKEN BOOTH

See how it was with those who came before,
how it will be with those who are living.
Like corn mortals ripen and fall;
like corn they come up again.
—Katha Upanishad - Part 1, Verse 6

I sat down at a chicken joint last night, and in the booth beside me was a mother and daughter. The girl was high school-aged, crying over something in pitch and tone that sounded like the end of the world but, in words and reality, was quite trivial.

There's a podcaster I like that says, "The worst thing that ever happened to you is the worst thing that ever happened to you." It really clicked in, seeing these two generations side-by-side. Whatever some other girl said to the boy this girl liked was the worst thing ever. Meanwhile, her mother, with four times the go-rounds on earth, has probably been through divorce settlements, health complications, financial woes, or a hundred other things that would put this high school drama to shame.

Fortunately for the daughter, the mother had the patience to sympathize with this social tragedy. I myself might have reached across the table to give her shoulders a good shake as I yell, "There are so many worse things coming down the line!" But that's just me.

It's amazing to look back at a number of events that felt like yesterday and realize those might've been the worst thing that ever happened to me too. Perhaps this mother could recognize herself in her daughter, going through the same cycle of trials she once went through before.

But life keeps pushing the threshold of "worst" further and further, making our tolerance higher. I'm sure in every painful situation we go through in life, we wish it wasn't happening. But if it didn't, we'd be the ones sitting across from our daughters while crying over boys, and they'd be reaching over a chicken sandwich to give us the violent shake.

That's all for now, but I'll leave you with this: Endure the trials of today, knowing you'll look back tomorrow and think they weren't so bad. Or maybe you will. As a friend's dad once told us at an impressionable young age, "Life sucks, and then you die." So eat as many tasty sandwiches as you can between now and then because it'll all be over soon.

FAMILY GAME NIGHT

Remember the Sabbath day, to keep it holy.
—Exodus 20:8

My gym philosopher buddy and I were half-jokingly pondering over whether "normal," family-game-night-type families actually exist.

"I don't know any of those people," he said. "None of my friends had that."

"Yeah," I said, "that's because you spend all your time here, surrounded by others working on insecurities instilled by their dysfunctional families. You know where all the 'normal' people are?"

"Where?"

"At family game night! With a self-confidence that doesn't require the pursuit of an improving physique because Mommy and Daddy instilled the belief that they're good enough the way they are! And so they're out in the world, attracting lovers and money while operating under the belief system that they're lovable and deserve the world, repelling *losers* like you, while you're attracting your own dysfunctional kind!"

Hardy har har, but I do wonder if there's any degree of truth to that, as opposed to "normal" families remaining a myth. I suppose it's more likely they just exist on one end of the bell curve while the rest of families fall somewhere in between. It seems like most people you encounter are driven by lingering insecurities instilled by imperfect upbringings, and the more I examine my own subconscious stories, the more I wonder who could have escaped their past without any ghosts hovering over their shoulder. This, too, I imagine, has a haunted house-like bell curve associated with it.

I will say one likable thing I've discovered in studying religions is the tradition in Judaism to have a Friday night family dinner, followed by a Sabbath with no internet, no phones, no cars, and just some good old rest and relaxation with the fam. What else is there to do in the absence of technology and transportation but to sit down around a Scrabble board and converse with members of your household?

If you're one of these perfectly functional beings who exist at that fringe of the function bell curve, please drop me a line at SeekingFamilyGameNightFamilies@gmail.com. I'd love to sit in on a rousing game of Parcheesi and observe what it's like.

STINKY ROOMMATES

The mindful ones exert themselves.
They are not attached to any home.
Like swans that abandon the lake,
they leave home after home behind.
—The Dhammapada - Chapter 7, Verse 91

This is the first time since I was eighteen that I've slept in the same bed for more than a year. The winds of change seem to blow in a rhythm where I've been uprooted annually. Often, the motivations for moving were not so much out of desire but necessity.

For example, I was once the first renter of a two-bedroom apartment, when the landlord found a second renter after I had moved in. The guy himself was nice enough, but for some reason, an absolutely awful smell would seep out of his room and infect the common area.

If you saw a photo of his room, you'd think it appeared normal enough, but if that photo were a scratch-and-sniff sticker, boy, were you in for a surprise.

Anytime he left the apartment with his door open, I would immediately shut it. The closer you got to touching the door, the more it stung the nostrils, and I would wonder if his own nostrils had been damaged in some kind of nostril-damaging accident.

He once invited me into the stench cave to see something on his computer, and it was impossible to breathe. I wanted to shake him by the ears and scream, "Can you not even smell this!?" But instead, I spent extended periods holding my breath and apologizing to my lungs.

I questioned how this guy could even survive in such an offensive environment, but after a few weeks of tolerating this sensory assault, I decided I could not. The landlord was understanding when I told her why I'd be breaking my lease, but this was the moment in my life when I decided that the price of sharing an apartment with someone else was no longer worth the price of my sanity.

That powerful aroma was the catalyst for me to cough up enough cash to pay for privacy and peace of mind, and I've never looked back.

I share this with you only to say that sometimes the stinky roommates of life are a blessing in disguise—even if they're a very, very olfactorily offensive blessing in disguise.

#NamasteOutOfYourRoomThanks

GROWING UP

A monk's not deemed 'an Elder'
through hair that's turning grey.
If he's just matured in age, he's deemed 'matured-in-vain'.
—The Dhammapada - Chapter 19, Verse 260

I recently reunited with a group of friends I haven't seen in years. They looked sharp in their suits and ties, talking about the careers they had pursued and the children they had gone on to raise. I couldn't believe how much they'd all grown up.

I remember what degenerates we were on college nights like it was yesterday. For example, one year, the bathroom in our dorm was on one end of the hall, while two of my friends lived down the other. On nights after drinking, J was too lazy to walk down the hall, so instead, he'd pee in bottles or jars or whatever was within reach when nature called.

The morning after one such night, I stumbled into their room to inquire about breakfast and found J dangling a Ziplock bag full of dark yellow liquid over his roommate's head. B sat with his arms crossed in a chair, mid-conversation with another friend of ours. I made eye contact with J as he lowered the bag, and it morphed to fit the shape of B's head. Without so much as turning around, needing no clarification of what just happened, B calmly said, "That's gross, man. It's still warm." J simply giggled as he raised it up and plopped it down again repeatedly, the sound of urine sloshing about in B's ear. College normalized this kind of behavior it seems.

On a separate occasion, we were at the beach, with eight of us standing in a circle and chatting. Mid-sentence, a trickle of liquid streamed down J's leg and moistened the sand between his feet. There was an awkward pause before his girlfriend said, "Are you *peeing*!?"

The world his litter box, J simply replied, "What? That's what you *do* at the beach."

She went on to marry him, and now they have a child.

These are the parents of America's youth today. As I keep that in mind, I look back on the role models I looked up to in my own childhood, wondering what kinds of pasts they had while I blindly saw them as authority figures. Surely, those generations who emerged from the sixties through the eighties have stories of their own, buried beneath careers and fancy clothing.

Degenerates raising degenerates: that's what's going on here. And someday I'm sure to join the ranks, keeping secrets from future generations behind a facade of maturity.

ARCHERY LESSONS

The Master said,
"A true teacher is one who,
keeping the past alive,
is also able to understand the present."
—*Analects of Confucius - Book 2, Chapter 11*

When I first learned to shoot archery, I signed up for group lessons. Our instructor was a jolly, round fellow who couldn't have been nicer. Though not athletic in appearance, he exuded the air of a master archer in character. For example, he wore league shirts and spoke the language of archery with fluency.

There was, however, a mixed bag of talent among the students. The best part was that we'd shoot at foam blocks encased in wood, so when someone missed terribly, there'd be a loud *bang!* as their arrow smashed into it. When missed just right, the arrow would bounce off the wood and come skittering back toward the shooter, which was awesome to see.

After we all got the hang of shooting at twenty yards, our instructor challenged us to step back to thirty. I was up first with my compound bow and honed in through the peep sight, zipping my shot straight into the bullseye. It felt great to do so in front of the teacher I so admired.

"You know," he said, borrowing a recurve bow from another student's hands, "I was never much for using sights when it came to hunting. I was always more of an instinctual shooter." This meant he would hunt the old-fashioned way, like a tribesman who relied on this ancient skill for survival.

As he stepped up to the line, tension filled the air, as there was a collective realization that we'd never actually seen the master in action, until now. He drew in a deep breath, raised the bow, drew it back, and held it steady. Time slowed as we observed an artist at work, his laser focus impressing us all.

Finally, he released it.

Bang! The arrow came skittering back to the line, the only sound in an otherwise silent room.

There was a long pause where we all stared at the result.

"Well," he finally broke the silence, handing the bow back to the girl he had borrowed it from, "I haven't gone hunting in quite some time."

PIGEON WENCH

While standing by a river,
the Master said,
"What passes away is, perhaps, like this.
Day and night it never lets up."
—*Analects of Confucius - Book 9, Chapter 17*

"Hello!" a voice rang out from nowhere.

"Hellooo!" it yelled again as two grannies sought to find where it came from.

"Hi, yeah, up here," a middle-aged woman called down toward their wheelchairs.

As the elderly women craned their necks to see who was screeching from above, the woman leaned over her balcony and said, "I know you mean well, but feeding bread to those birds leads to wing deformities!"

Why, if I had my bow, I woulda slung an arrow in her general direction, harassing people who have one foot in the grave like that.

"You listen to me, lady!" I wanted to yell. "If those old-timers wanna toss the remaining scraps of their social security at ducks, then you leave 'em alone!"

I didn't have to, though, as those sweet geriatrics ignored the wench and went on feeding. (That, or they were too deaf to understand what she was saying.)

By some cosmic intervention, this waterside scene occurred as I was reading the quote above, serving as a reminder that old age will eventually catch up with all of us.

Fortunately, I read Seneca's *On the Shortness of Life* when I was young and always kept in mind the essence of his work: "It is not that we have a short time to live, but that we waste a lot of it. Life is long enough, and a sufficiently generous amount has been given to us for the highest achievements if it were all well invested. But when it is wasted in heedless luxury and spent on no good activity, we are forced at last by death's final constraint to realize that it has passed away before we knew it was passing."

His wisdom made me realize how the existence we often take for granted is in short supply. We have, what, eighty years if we're lucky? And there's a chunk on the front end, which is barely remembered, and a chunk on the back end, which is, well, probably barely remembered. So, from the moment I read that book, I vowed to live my lively years by asking, "What's the most efficient use of my time right now?"

And if that means feeding wildlife when I'm half-dead, then you let me be.

EGYPTIAN NUISANCE

*Don't speak evil against each other,
dear brothers and sisters.
[...]
What right do you have to judge your neighbor?
—James 4:11-12*

There's a neighbor in my apartment complex who likes to feed the wildlife: ducks, geese, the occasional squirrel. One morning, I went out to the mailbox, and there she was, walking her dog with a fanny pack full of peanuts and breadcrumbs. Surrounding her was this gaggle of Egyptian geese that I truly, utterly despise.

It was kind of cute when two adults were raising six peeping goslings, but now that they're fully grown, it's just honk, honk, honk all the damn time. I wouldn't have it in me to stomp on a nest full of eggs myself, but if we wound back the clock knowing what they'd turn into and I heard a rumor of some who did? Well...

Before you get all judgy, look up a video of what these wretched monsters sound like and loop that on repeat from now until you go insane. Maybe you'll get a taste of what it's like to have it seeping through your windows all day.

To validate my feelings further, Florida Fish & Wildlife puts no limit on how many of these invasive creatures you can blast into oblivion. Just pow, pow, pow, and no one bats an eye. Meanwhile, kill one too many of the native ducks here, and they'll slap a *big* fine on your behind. So, take that into perspective.

"I hope you weren't trying to sleep!" said Duck Woman, tossing breadcrumbs directly below my bedroom window.

In my head, I thought some R-rated version of, *I really wish you wouldn't do that.* But out loud, I said, "Nooo. Who needs sleep anyway?"

"Trying to get a peanut to a squirrel is like trying to thread a needle!" she told me, tossing a wildly thrown shell in the general vicinity of the furry varmint. It bounced off the hood of some car with a clunk as one of the geese chased the squirrel away and gobbled it up.

"I see what you mean," I told her, faking whatever sympathy I could muster.

After collecting my mail, I went back inside and looked up foods that are toxic to geese. Turns out, peanuts are at the top of the list. I think I'll keep that bit of information to myself for now.

The truth is, I try not to judge others, I really do. But some people just plain deserve judgment. I mean, who in their right mind wears a fanny pack?

CONTEMPORARY "ART" MUSEUM

*He who checks rising anger
as a charioteer checks a rolling chariot,
him I call a true charioteer.
Others only hold the reins.*
—*The Dhammapada - Chapter 17, Verse 222*

A friend of mine showed me a contemporary "art" museum yesterday. You'd understand why I put "art" in quotation marks if you were there. Let's put it this way: The piece that stuck out the most was a giant Walmart receipt for some unmemorable purchase, blown up to the scale of a small coffin, lying haphazardly on the floor. (Don't ask why that's the comparison that came to mind. Perhaps a subconscious belief that's where this person's artistic aspirations belong.)

The "art" exhibit next to this tripping hazard was nothing but a sign that read, "Do not touch," which made me wonder if the juxtaposition was to imply you should touch the receipt. Was this part of the contemporariness of it all? I'm still unsure.

Maybe I'm a simpleton who believes art takes time, effort, and passion—not a three-dollar purchase you scan at your local print shop and blow up with the push of a button. When I think of art, I think of the Mona Lisa. What might da Vinci think of an oversized display of something you'd throw in the trash?

Surely it couldn't have been so bad, you say? Well, most of the other "art" required you to strain your eyes because theyweremostlyabunchofpieceswithwordssmushedtogetherlike thisbecauseapparentlythat'sartnow. Or they were giant, bloody, glass stalagmite-looking towers with a sign that read, "Trode!"—whatever that means.

The first piece in the first room was a vase with a giant erection. This was also the first and last sexual piece in the entire gallery, and frankly, it was all downhill from there. And doubly frankly, when I decided this was the first and last contemporary art museum I'd see.

What does this have to do with Buddhism, you ask? Absolutely nothing, other than the fact that I had to reflect on why this "art" being on display for a $15 admission made me so angry. I'll let you know if I ever find the answer.

But then again, without it, I wouldn't have had the inspiration for this post, now would I?

I guess there's light after all. #ArtistsInspiringArtists

MOUNT TRASHMORE

Eat and drink freely, but do not waste.
Verily, [God] does not love the wasteful.
—*The Qur'an - 7:31*

Let's talk dirty for a minute: Landfills.

We've all seen those clips of trash piles falling into the ocean, seagulls plucking through garbage, fish swimming through rubbish, baby otters with a six-pack ring around their necks.

I just have one question: Whose idea was it to put a landfill on waterfront property anyway?

Shouldn't that real estate have been used for a condo or a golf course?

What, the garbage men needed a prime view from their office suite?

Why don't we dump that shit in Nebraska, or Oklahoma, or some other state with a useless desert? Who saw a coral reef and said, "I think I'll put my waste management facility here." We've got a million square miles of uninhabitable wasteland in this country, and someone thought it wise to litter what could have been a beach resort? That's the most un-American business model I've ever heard of.

Imagine if we shipped all our trash to one central location and piled it so high we could build a Mount Rushmore on top of it. Imagine the stench. Imagine the revulsion. Imagine the number of loonies worldwide who would pay to see such an atrocity. Now *that's* a business plan!

"Come one, come all, and witness the grand Trash Mountain!"

We could build an amusement park around it, with roller coasters zooming over piles of debris, trolley rides circling flaming methane geysers, and raft rides down sewage runoff rapids. Vendors could sell clothespins, gas masks, and tetanus shots. Museums could feature notable celebrity discards. There could be 'pick your own souvenirs' extravaganzas. The possibilities are endless.

Yet here we are, squandering potential, throwing away the chance, wasting opportunities.

Vote for me in the coming election, and I'll make sure your dirtiest dreams come true, all while saving the oceans.

What does this have to do with religion, you ask? Well, it seems the time to merge church and state for the betterment of the planet has arrived. It's time to put my face on Mount Trashmore.

ICE MAKER OBVIOUSNESS

When it's cold, you can move around to stay warm.
When it's hot, you should keep still and stay cool.
But whatever the weather, if you stay calm,
the world will sort itself out around you.
—*Tao Te Ching, Verse 45*

The first words in my new ice maker instruction manual were, "WARNING: You could be killed or seriously injured if you don't <u>immediately</u> follow the instructions."

My mind raced past the motivation for this ingeniously subtle form of Chinese warfare and into the potential fate of any victim foolish enough to mishandle such an appliance. Have rates of hypothermic death been on the rise since the development of this technology? Does lethal refreshment claim you after drinking room-temperature liquid your entire life? Are people dying of boredom while watching ice being made? Or is the first inclination of most to strip off the rubber coating around the wire and hold on tight as they plug it into the wall? The reasonable number of possibilities seemed endless.

Whatever the cause of early demise, I avoided it by reading the instruction manual—immediately, thank God—and now I've been enjoying the benefits of morning ice baths in my own home. And let me tell you: This is the way. Better than any cup of coffee. Better than Motrin for aches and pains. Better than motivational mantras you might be using to start your day. Remaining calm in the face of cold conditions: That's the way to be. That said, if I ever neglect the instruction manual, I'll be sure to tell your grandchildren hello after they cryogenically defrost me like Austin Powers.

Stay cool, my friends.

IGUANA SNIPER

*A good traveler has no fixed plans
and is not intent upon arriving.*
—*Tao Te Ching - Verse 27*

As you'd expect from any late-night Miami Uber driver, this one shared stories that could only emerge from such a city. Like the man who casually revealed a baggy of cocaine for a quick snort on the highway. Or the teen who pulled a knife on her mother over a squabble about a boyfriend. Or the gentleman who drunkenly punched his wife in the face over something trivial.

In the midst of these joyful taxi tales, he laughed to interject the conversation with this: "I used to work at this country club, and they hired a former Army sniper to shoot the iguanas! Can you believe that?"

As unbelievable as an iguana sniper may be, I was so thrown off by the transition that I had no response but to blink. I'm not sure if he just needed to get that off his chest or what, but he got back on track as quickly as he got off it, telling me a story about a couple he'd picked up who'd totaled a rental car by swerving into a barrier on the highway. As any rational person might, he assumed they were in need of a lift to the rental car HQ when they called, or perhaps the police station, or maybe even a hospital. But instead, it turned out the drop-off location was a local 24/7 bar that lived up to its reputation at 6 a.m. on a Sunday.

In his heavy Turkish accent, he told me, "Nighttime is not the right time."

We laughed at the summary of his highlight reel, followed by an awkward pause as we approached my terminal. Deadpan, I filled it with this: "You don't mind if I do some heroin before my flight, do you?"

The tension grew as he stared ahead, calculating whether or not I was joking. And because I love messing with people I'll never see again, I let out a heavy sigh and said, "I'll take that as a no."

What? I gave him a nice tip.

I know this has little to do with the quote above, other than the fact I was traveling. Sue me. But I thought it was funny, and perhaps there's a lesson about planning to be cautious during travels if you are intent on arriving. You never know if someone's on drugs, has a knife, or is an ex-military iguana sniper.

Stay safe out there.

UBER DRIVER MADNESS

Your worldly goods [...] are but a trial and a temptation, whereas with God there is a tremendous reward.
—*The Qur'an - 64:15*

When I first climbed into the Uber, and the man with a Middle Eastern accent dove straight into road rage stories, I was a tad alarmed. Apparently, his fiancée doesn't like it when he throws his coffee out the window at jaywalkers and then proceeds to yell at them to the point where they aim a gun at his face. She *really* doesn't like it when he eggs them on further by saying, "Go ahead. Shoot me. Shoot me!"

Allegedly. You know how these Uber drivers can be, embellishing stories to the point of sounding braggadocious.

"Oh, stop it," I said. "You weren't that brave."

But he's from New York, where that's just another Monday.

The knots in my stomach unfurled when somehow he segued this into a tear-jerker about his first wife dying of Covid there, then getting laid off from his job all in the same week.

"But that's life," he said, brushing it off like a fender bender he'd buffed out over the weekend. That's when it all made sense, where this road rage came from.

Pre-pandemic, he found himself working for the king of Saudi Arabia in his home country. The money was as good as you could imagine, but the moment he witnessed his king murder another employee just for refusing to perform a job, he decided it was time to rethink his career.

"I feel much safer in America," he told me, sharing how he fled the country because quitting wasn't really an option. Unfortunately, this displeased the king, who then dissolved the equivalent of $2 million that my driver had saved up in his account. And as it turns out, lawyers can't do much in the face of royal injustice.

"It's alright," he said. "Money can't save you. I was better off starting over here anyway."

Better to be a broke freeman than a rich prisoner, is the lesson I derived from that little tale.

And so my ride ended with me strolling into the airport toward vacation because no king has the power to wipe my financial slate clean. But I suppose that God can do this anytime is the big reminder of this little School of Life episode.

PROCREATION LIMITATION

The father who does not teach his son his duties
is equally guilty with the son who neglects them.
—Attributed to Confucius, unconfirmed source

The fact that there's no test to determine whether or not you should be allowed to have children is mind-boggling. I, for one, think a standardized test should be issued worldwide before any more procreation happens.

Who would monitor whether or not those who failed actually abstained from multiplying, you ask? Excellent question. However, logistics are above my pay grade; I'm simply the idea guy.

Sticking to what falls within my wheelhouse, though, here's an example question for our little parental quality screening exam:

Under any circumstance whatsoever, would you even consider allowing your child to bring what sounds like a squeaky dog toy onto a red-eye flight where others are trying to sleep?

The answer choices would be something like:

A) Yes

B) No

C) I am a complete and utter moron

The irony is that I saw seat number 13F—the last available window seat that I assumed would allow me to get some shut-eye—and I splurged on the extra seat selection fee while poo-pooing that myth of bad luck. But not only did seat number 13 turn out to be unlucky, but the F apparently stood for something like, "Why don't you take your plan to sleep and you go *Fuck* yourself."

Question #2:

If your child was screeching like a howler monkey, while kicking and banging on the back of someone else's seat, would you:

A) Calmly explain to them that such behavior is unacceptable in a civilized society.

B) Give them a quick slap upside the head.

C) Encourage them to take off their shoes so that a putrid stench emanates throughout the plane.

Now, at this point in our fertility privilege test, if you've chosen C for either question, your testicles or ovaries would immediately be removed, because there's just no place for genes like yours in our newly monitored gene pool.

I would have come up with more questions, but quite frankly, I got a bit queasy from the smell and couldn't think straight after that. That said, I'm not sure more than the two questions above are really necessary.

Alas, until the day this ingenious plan takes flight, happy procreating.

HAMBURGERS & BUREACRACY

Matters of justice get lost in red tape and bureaucracy.
—*Ecclesiastes 5:8*

In the foggy recess of my mind lurks the vision of a playground near Grandma's house. This aging recreation area may have suffered from simpler architecture, but it offered what no other playground ever did: a hamburger tower.

That's right: a two-story ladder in the middle of four poles holding up a hollow, metal delicacy.

The thrills of climbing this classic American delight were as delectable as the views; the joys of shouting down to a smaller Granny were more scrumptious than any scholastic achievement.

You can't imagine the depth of disappointment that replaced the height of anticipation the first time I saw Hamburger Tower was gone. We heard they removed it because too many kids got stuck up there, afraid to climb down the way they came.

Losers, always ruining the best things for others.

Some schmuck with a fear of heights can't figure out how to get down, so *I'm* grounded from the thrills of visiting Grandma?

Where's the justice in this world?

Why must the competent suffer others' incompetence?

Since when do we curb the construction of society to fit the limits of the inept and the shameful?

I mean, what kind of irresponsible guardian thought it wise to let Jimmy "Butter Fingers" climb a two-story ladder anyway?

And how about we start with a CAUTION sign that reads, "Not for morons or the faint of heart"?

What am I supposed to do now: scratch my itch for heights on the seesaw?

That tower was a monument to brave children everywhere. Kids like me came from miles away to experience the ascension into those recreational heights.

Instead of the fittest surviving, we force the brave and the able to lower their standards to those of the cowards and the nincompoops. It's anti-Darwinism, is what it is.

I say let the Hamburger Towers of the world stand tall, and whoever gets stuck up there rot of starvation in the most ironic fashion.

Why should the capable be deprived of challenge?

Why should the adventurous be tamed?

Why should those of us with a grip as sure as Elmer's be subject to the demolition of the playgrounds we love?

I thought this was America! *Fuck* Jimmy "Butter Fingers."

BOO-BOO-RU

*Do you have the patience to wait
till your mud settles and the water is clear?
Can you remain unmoving
till the right action arises by itself?*
—*Tao Te Ching - Verse 15*

I recently bought a Certified Pre-Owned vehicle that was only two years old and had very few miles on it. It was essentially brand new, or so the greasy sales rep told me.

The problems started the day I drove it off the lot, beginning with a window that wouldn't roll up properly after being lowered. I drove 45 minutes back to the dealership the next day, at which point they did a "program reset," flickering the switch some combination of up and down for some combination of seconds. My initial thought was, *Do they pre-program a system reset in anticipation of the window failing by design?* But anyway, the window was fixed—for about twenty-four hours, that is, until the issue returned, and I had to drive back again.

They insisted that the "re-programming" was the solution, which it was, for about twenty-four hours. I wasn't keen on making that same drive so soon, but fortunately for me, the "brand new" car battery began failing a month later, stranding me in various places and giving me another reason to return.

After the new battery was replaced and the window pointlessly re-programmed once more, the replacement battery died two months later. Did I mention the main counsel pooped out somewhere in between? So they had to ship a new one from Japan, requiring another trip to the dealership. Oh, then the cables connected to the replacement battery began draining the replacement battery excessively, so those had to be replaced.

At this point, I insisted the window unit be replaced as well, because it was clear that re-programming was nothing but a sham. After they called me in once the window parts had arrived, they were nice enough to keep me waiting for only two hours before they informed me that the parts technician had ordered the wrong parts for the door, and that I'd have to come back again.

Incompetence is usually a trigger of mine, but at that point, I just laughed—which either signifies the remarkable personal growth I've experienced over the course of owning the vehicle for a year, or it's the first sign of insanity. I'm not sure which.

Despite what the quote above suggests, there's not really a lesson about patience here. The real lesson is that sometimes life bends you over, and that's that.

ACIDIC ILLUSIONS

*Having heard the supremely confidential spiritual knowledge,
which You have revealed out of compassion for me,
my illusion is now dispelled.*
—*The Bhagavad Gita - Chapter 11, Verse 1*

My friend once told me the story of how Ram Dass went to India and supplied a Hindu guru with three tabs of LSD. The man allegedly took them all at once, yet showed no signs of being affected by this potent substance. The implication was that this man was already *so* enlightened that modern "medicine" had no impact on him whatsoever. He apparently lived in the state of mind that LSD typically induces in the human psyche.

I thought about it for a moment before I said, "You mean to tell me this guy perceived the world through a vision of constantly shape-shifting distortions and purple glasses, where the world is dominated by specific colors for hours? Or is it possible that the Acid-gobbling guru was unaffected because his brain chemistry didn't react to that chemical, just like some people are unaffected by consuming marijuana while others drift off into another universe?"

Perhaps Ram Dass was unaware of such possibilities at the time, blinded by the notion that someone could ingest a dose of LSD that would knock any normal person on their ass. And like anyone prone to good storytelling might do, he crafted this fable around someone he revered, someone seemingly capable of something he didn't understand.

I doubt that anyone can be so spiritually "above" LSD that they walk away unaffected by an otherwise reliable shift in consciousness. Give that same man a heroic dose of mushrooms, however, or enough DMT to blast him into another dimension, and maybe the initial perspective of Dass would be washed away by the guru's exposure to a different chemical.

My friend agreed that this story served as a good example of how we can become blinded by the allure of a legend, and this was a valuable reminder for me to continue searching for any of my own beliefs that can be dissolved by an alternate perspective.

PLAY THE GAME

*Fools dwelling in ignorance,
yet imagining themselves wise and learned,
go round and round in crooked ways,
like the blind led by the blind.*
—Katha Upanishad - Part 2, Verse 5

I stumbled upon this quote yesterday: "Who are you to be such a committed advocate of a faith that's so complex that there's no way that someone like you could understand it?"

The question doesn't just apply to religion, but any topic, really. I see it in my personal life, professional settings, and in public. People are willing to take a stance on a topic, whether they have a wealth of supporting evidence to back it up or not. That fascinates me.

Belief systems, for many people, seem to be built on a shaky foundation of buzzwords, phrases, platitudes, or things they heard from someone else. The best part is they don't even bother to further reinforce this foundation by looking into their stance any further. But challenge them with a few probing questions, and they'd rather dig their heels into the dirt of ignorance and double down on enthusiasm for their "team" than search for the truth.

As for me, my approach to an argument (or stimulating conversation with differing views, as I like to call it) is this: "I'm not saying you're wrong, I'm just asking you to show me why you're right." I'm more interested in finding out why you're holding onto your beliefs than proving one of us "right" or "wrong." Most people aren't even willing to play the game, though. It's deflect or shut down or point behind you and say, "Look over there!"

Why are people so afraid to claim ignorance about a topic they're unknowledgeable about? It never made any sense to me, as I have no trouble taking at least a partially neutral stance on a topic which I know little about. But maybe I'd rather just stand my ground in a field of ignorance than wander round and round like the blind leading the blind.

WAR PAINT

Elevate yourself through the power of your mind,
and not degrade yourself,
for the mind can be the friend and also the enemy of the self.
—*The Bhagavad Gita - Chapter 6, Verse 5*

I've been reading what's been dubbed a modern spiritual classic: *I Am That* by Sri Nisargadatta Maharaj. In a chapter on meditation, he says, "We are slaves to what we do not know; what we know, we are masters." He was referring to using meditation in search of voices inside ourselves that offer weakness, so we can understand their causes and discover their workings. I thought he put it aptly when describing how "the unconscious dissolves when brought into conscious" because, on many occasions, I've found this dissolution feels like a tangible release of pent-up energy.

In the next line of the Bhagavad Gita quoted above, Krishna tells Arjun that "for those who have conquered the mind, it is their friend. For those who have failed to do so, the mind works like an enemy." In recent years, I've gone on the ruthless search for unconscious stories that are no longer serving me, and yesterday, the term "trauma hunting" popped into mind. I feel this term brings forth the image of an Arnold Schwarzenegger-like figure in war paint, trouncing through the jungles of the subconscious in search of metaphorical Predators. And while ancient scriptures like the one referenced above can guide us in the right direction, only we can put on the war paint and slash through the jungle.

When you begin to dissolve those limiting beliefs by shining conscious awareness on them, you become less of who you are and more of who you could be. We alone are responsible for our own elevation or degradation in this regard. So, happy hunting, my friends.

PLANTAR FASCIITIS

*Can a man walk on burning coals
without scorching his feet?
—Proverbs 6:28*

I've dealt with plantar fasciitis on and off since I was a teenager. I've tried to mitigate the pain with heat, ice, stretching, foam rolling, acupuncture, red light therapy, or anything else you can think of, but nothing has had a lasting effect. Never in my dreams would I imagine this might be the topic that popped into mind two hours into a recent float tank session, but there it was.

I realized this chronic ailment started sometime during my track career in high school when I was placed in an event at which I had no chance of excelling. What came to mind as I began to feel tension in my legs and feet release was this idea that plantar fasciitis was a physical manifestation of an ego-protective mechanism for coming in last (or close to last) during races, so I'd have some kind of excuse to lean on.

Boom. Chew on that for a moment.

As a kinesiology major, I bought into the paradigm that things like stretching were the key to long-lasting mobility. However, the more I experience emotional shifts from practices like meditation and myofascial release, the more I think these chronic issues stem from deep psychological wounds that can only be accessed during certain states of consciousness.

Part of the reason I left that field of study is because I recognized a ceiling of limitation with physical manipulation of the body, whereas true healing, I've found, begins by delving into the mind.

It's been a few weeks now since that experience, and I've powered through workouts that might otherwise cause discomfort or pain, so I'm optimistic this mental shift was the key.

PLANTAR FASCIITIS 2

Indeed what is to come
will be better for you than what has gone by.
—The Qur'an 93:4

My left hip has always felt kind of stiff, and I wondered if it was a case similar to my plantar fasciitis while discussing it with a friend at the gym. I didn't consciously intend to find out, but last night I woke up from a dream of getting into a fight with my dad over something trivial.

It wasn't a real memory, but the feelings it stirred in me led me to reflect on actual memories. Like the time on the boat when my cousins were allowed to have fun catching lots of sunfish with my uncle while my dad made me join him on the other side of the boat to pursue some less fruitful bass fishing. They went on giggling, catching many "silly" fish, while the joy was sucked right out of that trip when I had to pursue this more elusive and "serious" fish.

I also relived a night after my parents' divorce when my father scolded me for fooling around at the dinner table, and I was forced to embody this sense that I needed to take life a little more seriously. The fun was sucked right out of me there too.

In fact, both of my parents' reactions to the divorce seeped into my newly-formed belief system that life wasn't fun, and that you had to be serious to survive. This "serious" attitude has permeated every aspect of my life. Even my seemingly ironic pursuits of improv and stand-up comedy have become "serious" studies of silly art forms, while their very essence is about letting go and having fun.

All this reflection occurred as the tension in my hip unwound in a way I hope will provide the kind of lasting relief I've experienced with my feet.

Bada-boom. All aboard the midnight train to trauma town! Next stop, fun town ;)

DON'T BE AN ALBATROSS

Few among men are those who cross to the farther shore.
The rest, the bulk of men,
only run up and down the hither bank.
—The Dhammapada - Chapter 6, Verse 85

The Laysan albatross is born flightless, relying on its parents to bring it food in the early stages of life. But at some point, the parents stop coming, and the adolescent bird is left to fend for itself. The only way to get nourishment then is to fly out to sea and find it for itself.

The bird is so large, however, that it requires proper wind conditions for takeoff, especially for its first flight with undeveloped wings. So it waits for the gusts to be just right before speed-waddling down the beach like a runway, flapping as hard as it can while praying to make it at least as far as the open ocean.

Why? Because lurking beneath the surface are migratory tiger sharks who have arrived to prowl the shallows, knowing the first flight of many a young albatross doesn't last very long. And for those that don't, because the winds of fate decided to die down, for example, well... chomp, chomp.

Imagine being recently abandoned by your parents, hungry beyond belief, and feebly reliant on undeveloped wings to survive. Now, you must take your first flight over shark-infested waters in order not to starve. Ahh, nature.

What does this have to do with the above quote, you ask? Well, perhaps we've all been hesitant at times to leave the land of comfort for fear of what lurks within the proverbial shark-infested waters. But casting away that fear is the only way to leave the shores of starvation and venture out into the world where growth and prosperity are possible.

I write this only to say that whatever possible reality you face, at least you're not an albatross.

That is all.

LITTER BUGS

Then your light will break forth like the dawn,
and your healing will quickly appear;
then your righteousness will go before you,
and the glory of the Lord will be your rear guard.
—Isaiah 58:8

I've been living within a short driving distance of the beach for six months now and haven't gone to the shore for a single sunrise. Don't ask me how. I could list a bunch of excuses—like being busy, preoccupied, or having a schedule that caused me to sleep in late—but the point is, I was missing out.

Anyway, the first word that came to mind as the morning's rays pierced over the horizon was "glory." God's glory, I suppose.

The second word that came to mind was "assholes," as all the trash left behind by people the day before was illuminated.

What dicks, I thought. But then I saw a retirement-aged man walking down the beach with a litter-picker, and I thought, *You know, if there weren't such assholes in the world, then there wouldn't be much good for the do-gooders to do, now would there?*

Those are God's dicks. Those are God's assholes. Providing balance in the world. They are the night's darkness to the morning's light. Without litter droppers, litter pickers would have no litter to pick. They are the reason good deeds can be done, the reason retirement-aged glory exists.

#LetThatSinkIn

And so, as I left the beach that beautiful morning, I did my part and cast my plastic water bottle straight into the sea.

YA KNOW?

The best are like water,
bringing help to all without competing.
Choosing what others avoid,
they thus approach the Tao.
—*The Tao Te Ching - Verse 8*

Yesterday, I did a thing: I bought a surfboard.

I just bought one. (Used, of course, I'm not a madman). It didn't even occur to me until afterward that maybe I should rent one first, or take a lesson to see if I might like it. Those thoughts didn't sink in until after the surfboard was running the length of my SUV, partially blocking my view out the window on the way to the beach. I didn't even check to see if it was high tide.

It wasn't. But I went in and fumbled around like a fool for a while anyway (after the lifeguard blew his whistle at me, shooing me off to the other side of the pier to "surf" the nonexistent waves in the designated area. How embarrassing). It felt a bit like wrestling an alligator. As far as I know, wrestling alligators isn't a prerequisite for surfing, but as someone who's never taken lessons, don't take my word for it.

I felt even more foolish floundering around on a surfboard at low tide in front of a bunch of random people. I kept wondering, *What is everyone thinking about me right now?* Then

I realized they weren't, nobody was. And if they were, it was probably something along the lines of, *Huh. There's a guy with a surfboard.* Or even if they were thinking, *Look at that idiot floundering about on a surfboard at low tide*, who cares. The timing in life for impulsively floundering around on a surfboard at low tide just felt right, ya know? The timing didn't feel so right when I was living in Colorado, ya know? Then people would've been justified in thinking, *What is this idiot doing floundering about on a surfboard?* Ya know?

After that, I felt a little less foolish. I felt a little more like a random guy at the beach struggling on a surfboard because that's where us random guys with surfboards go. To the beach. To struggle. To fight the good fight. To commit ourselves to impulse buys that should've been rentals. To choose failing in front of strangers like others might avoid. To willingly drip down toward the lowest of places. To approach the Tao with the yielding nature of water. Ya know?

SURFING AT SUNRISE

The Master observes the world
but trusts his inner vision.
He allows things to come and go.
His heart is open as the sky.
—Tao Te Ching - Verse 12

I've been waking up in time to make it to the beach for sunrise, and the skies have been nothing short of paintings. This morning, I paddled out on the surfboard, and simply floating offshore as the sun came over the horizon made me feel closer to this phenomenon than I've ever been before. The thought, *Why haven't I been doing this all my life?* came to mind. Soon after that, I rode my first legitimate wave and was hooked on the lifestyle.

I lived in South Florida eight years prior, and I felt like this place chewed me up and spat me out. I was apprehensive to return, but opportunity knocked, and my intuition seemed to be calling me back, which I trusted.

Although the friends I thought I had here seemed to disappear, I let go of the attachment to my expectations, and new friends have come into the picture since then. I'm loving where I live more and more as the days go by, and, to quote the Tao's last line here, I try to keep my heart as open as the sky.

I attribute much of my shift in attitude and expectations to studying religions like Taoism. Ancient wisdom like "Observe the world but trust your inner vision" will never expire.

THOUGHTLESS BASTARDS 1

And remember Our servant Job,
when he called to his Lord,
"Satan has afflicted me with hardship and suffering."
[...]
And We restored his family,
and their like with them;
as a mercy from Us and a reminder for those of understanding.
—The Qur'an - 38:41-43

My backpack was stolen the other night. Brand new Osprey with my phone, keys, and wallet inside. I was surfing at sunset, and when I got in after dark, it was gone. At least they left my sandals...

I was pissed. I got all, "Woe is me," "I hate people," "The world has gone to shit," and I couldn't sleep thinking about how much money and effort I'd spend replacing those things.

The timing couldn't have been more perfect, while studying the Book of Job, philosophizing over why bad things happen to good people. As I lay in bed that night, seething, I reflected on all Job went through, losing everything, including his children and health. I, on the other hand, lost only a few material things that could easily be replaced, causing nothing more than an inconvenience that would pass within a few days. (I'm even smart enough to keep a spare car key under the tire well and a house key in a lockbox, so I wasn't even locked out.) I did, however, feel a lesson bubbling up that I should have known all along: Don't be so trusting of random strangers on the beach.

Except when I went back to the beach early the next morning to look for it one last time, I asked a fireman at the station across the street if he knew of any kind of Lost & Found. Or rather, I prefaced this would-be question with, "It's likely my backpack was just stolen, but—"

"Come with me," he cut me off, leading me into the garage. And there, sitting on a table between two fire trucks, was my backpack. "Some guy brought it in last night thinking it was left behind." My hatred of mankind immediately melted. "Thank God for good people," he said, "huh?"

Yes, well, something like that, Mr. Fireman.

Damn overly-ambitious do-gooders, leaving my sandals behind to get washed out to sea and whatnot. Thoughtless bastards...

THOUGHTLESS BASTARDS 2

In the secret cave of the heart, two are seated by life's fountain.
The separate ego drinks of the sweet and bitter stuff,
liking the sweet, disliking the bitter,
while the supreme Self drinks sweet and bitter,
neither liking this nor disliking that.
The ego gropes in darkness, while the Self lives in light.
So declare the illumined sages.
—Katha Upanishad - Part 3, Verse 1

When my bag was "stolen" (as mentioned in the prior post), my immediate emotion was anger. Often when emotions are triggered, I resort to journaling as a way to process them. I've found that the first step in moving past an emotion is to confront it head-on. Writing things down over the years has helped me do just that. Once they're off my chest and down on paper, it provides me with an opportunity to examine them from a bird's eye view and reflect upon the situation.

Here, after the initial outpour of blah, blah, blah, complain, complain, complain, I was able to process what happened from a centered state of being and realize, "I still have my health, a bed to sleep in tonight, and the means to replace the items I lost. Tomorrow, I'll begin that process and life will go on."

The very next morning, I happened to read one of Robert Greene's meditations in *The Daily Laws*, where he described this process perfectly: "It might be wise to use a journal in which you record your self-assessments with ruthless objectivity."

I loved that, ruthless objectivity. Centering yourself in a neutral position to observe your own actions is a necessary step toward detachment. By doing this repeatedly over the years, the process has become mostly second nature. When the emotional self rears its ugly head in the moment, I'm able to recognize it happening and pause to reflect on what's arising.

The ego is the enemy when it comes to unconsciously maintaining illusions, as described perfectly in the quote above with reference to disliking the bitter aspects of life in preference of the sweet. But the supreme Self drinks in the bitter and sweet of life all the same, to avoid groping in the darkness of angry emotions and living in the light of observing life for what it is.

This line of thinking also parallels the Taoist philosophy of wei-wu-wei—going with the flow of life—and I love to see similarities between religions.

DOCILITY

When the sun rises,
the moon is not visible.
Wherever spiritual wisdom appears,
ignorance is dispelled.
—Siri Guru Granth - Ang 791

"It's a secret the higher-ups trying to keep us docile don't want you to know," said the guy telling me I should stare directly at the sun. There may have been a caveat about doing it at sunrise when the sun is weak, but the point is this suppressed information was something I could capitalize on if I wanted to cleanse my pineal gland. "Like this," he added, clenching his fists while dropping into an athletic stance, sharing a squinty demonstration with the kind of tinfoil hat determination you'd expect from someone trying to go blind.

Apparently, the ancients used this gazing technique to "purify the mind" and "deepen psychic ability." The novice, though, "should practice in front of a candle first, then gradually build up to the sun."

When you say 'gradually build up,' I thought, *what does that mean exactly?*

A candle is the type of flame blown out with a single puff on your birthday. When a sun blows out, it has the potential to rip a hole in the universe. I couldn't help but wonder what the next stage of linear progression might look like.

A flame thrower?

A house fire?

A nuclear explosion?

I skipped every phase of progression for logistical reasons and went straight to the beach the next morning. Turns out I didn't dare stare directly into the rising orb for reasons of skeptical hesitation and/or government-inspired docility.

I rationalized my avoidance with the belief this practice had more to do with focusing on something to aid in meditation, exposure to Vitamin D-boosting rays, and being present with a scene that can inspire dopamine release.

Call me docile, but in the end, I chose to keep my pineal gland uncleansed at the risk of keeping my retinas intact. Something in me couldn't get over the notion that a modern game of telephone had convoluted the true purpose of this ancient practice, and it seems plausible that the ancients were unconcerned with combating the docility imposed by The Man.

That said, let the record show that I by no means wish to dissuade you from making pineal-cleansing choices. I believe in the freedom to walk the tightrope between anti-docility and blindness if you so choose.

YOU FREAK!

*Each separate being in the universe
returns to the common source.
Returning to the source is serenity.*
—*Tao Te Ching - Verse 16*

I've been pushing myself to meet at least one new person every day. Sometimes, I tell myself I'm going to introduce myself to someone, but when the moment arrives, I come up with excuses like, "She's too X," or "He's probably Y," or "I don't know what to say." It's when the opportunity slips by that I feel stupid, though.

What's the worst that could happen? They scream, "GET AWAY FROM ME, YOU FREAK!" Doubt it, especially if you're approaching with at least some semblance of normalcy. The worst is probably a quick brush-off, like, "I'm really busy right now," or "I'm meeting my [friend/colleague/spouse]," or "Mommy told me never to talk to strangers."

The approach I've been using lately is as simple as can be: a smile and the question, "Mind if I introduce myself?" So far, I haven't received a hard 'No,' but even if I do, I probably didn't want to meet that person anyway. Everyone I've approached has been warmly receptive, and one gal even told me, "It's nice to meet someone like this. Most people are always wrapped up in their phones."

Introduced myself to a young lady sitting by herself this morning and she mentioned coming for the sunrise with her boyfriend, but said he was off wandering around.

"Is he the jealous type?" I asked. "Should I leave?"

"He'll probably wanna shoot you," she said, pointing behind me. I was relieved to turn and see a guy walking around with a camera.

They turned out to be great, and we had a lot in common. We talked about religion, meditation, psychedelics, float tanks, ice baths, acupuncture, breathing techniques, and more.

One thing she said that felt relatable to the quote above was, "You can recognize who has seen God." Encountering other souls from the common source comes with an air of serenity, but sometimes you can miss them if you never stop to say hello. I almost didn't introduce myself. I almost made an excuse not to. But instead, a handshake sparked a solid conversation and served as a good reminder that there are wonderful people are out there waiting to meet you as well.

"WHY DO WE EVEN HAVE MOTHERS!?"

Focus not on the rudenesses of others,
not on what they've done or left undone,
but on what you have and haven't done yourself.
—*The Dhammapada - Chapter 4, Verse 50*

I met a woman the other morning who told me, "I held my phone up for an *hour* to take a time-lapse video of the sunrise for my mother, and when I sent it to her, all she sent back was a thumbs up." She laughed and said, "Why do we even have mothers!?"

There was laughter on the outside, but there was pain on the inside. All I could think about was how this disappointment comes down to failed expectations, wanting someone else to be something they're not.

I had a similar "failed expectations" moment flare up the other day when someone no-showed me last second without an explanation. I think all you can do is move others into a category of people with a different standard of ethics and behavior that better suits them, then continue upholding your own. Moping over wishing they were different doesn't help you, and it certainly won't change them. Lowering your expectations of everyone around doesn't do much good either. Simply observing who they are objectively is the way to go. Then, you'll appreciate those who align with your standards all the more.

Aim for that non-attachment.

"THIS ALWAYS HAPPENS TO ME!"

The wise,
realizing through meditation the timeless Self,
beyond all perception,
hidden in the cave of the heart,
leave pain and pleasure far behind.
—Katha Upanishad - Part 2, Verse 12

Thunderstorms are frequent and ferocious where I live, with rain whipping through the screened-in patio on which I sit. My first instinct is usually to duck inside to stay dry, but last time I remembered a story I once heard on a podcast. A father said that whenever there was a rainstorm, he would always take his son outside to experience the elements. He did this because he didn't want to ingrain the perception that rainy days were "bad." Now, that's a self-aware parent who realizes the influence they have in shaping a young child's mind.

It felt good to check in with the simpler pleasures of life—like the sound of water trickling down a gutter or streaks of lightning flashing through the sky. While feeling the spatter of raindrops as they filled the screen holes, I wondered what perceptions might have been blurred by my own early influences, kind of like the rain was blurring my view of the outside world now.

Certain people shape our worldview before we ever have a chance, and we form patterns of how we live out our lives. I've been on a mission to dig through every one of them I can recognize, questioning all of my self-limiting beliefs, ego-driven protective mechanisms, and inner dialogues that may be attracting negative things into my life.

Meditation helps dissect the root of any trigger of negative emotions so you can examine it with a magnifying glass. This process helps to clean the lens through which you see the world, mitigating some of the pain in your mind.

I witnessed another example of perceptions when I was sitting with someone on the beach recently. Out of nowhere, seagull poop plopped down from the sky onto her shoulder.

As I said, "What are the chances?" she said, "This always happens to me!"

As I said, "This always happens to you?" she said, "But my mother told me it's good luck."

I wanted to say, "Baby, I think your momma lied to you about having a target on your back because that's just shit luck," but I didn't, because perhaps there are some perceptions we might want to hold onto.

JAWS

*[The Master] understands that the universe
is forever out of control,
and that trying to dominate events
goes against the current of the Tao.*
—*Tao Te Ching - Verse 30*

I struck up a conversation with a stranger and went down a rabbit hole of childhood and psychology. Early on, she mentioned her favorite movie was *JAWS*, and that she had seen it over two hundred times.

"Two *hundred* times!?"

"Yeah," she said, "it's my comfort movie."

I thought the concept of having a horror film as a comfort movie was both bizarre and humorous. However, later in the conversation, she mentioned her parents getting divorced when she was around eight years old.

"Just out of curiosity, was this around the time your *JAWS* infatuation began?"

She thought about it for a moment before saying, "Yeah, I guess so."

"I wonder if there's any connection with the divorce, like watching a movie about chaos until you could predict every minute of it to the point you feel in control."

"Maybe," she said, shrugging her shoulders casually. "My parents' divorce was pretty messy... like a bloodbath, you might say."

What a strangely fascinating coping mechanism that would be if it's true. I'm picturing this poor girl curled up on the couch with a bowl of popcorn as her parents are screaming in the background, shark-infested waters becoming her go-to for serenity.

I'll need to reflect on my own past for similar coping mechanisms, but I'll have to look outside of the cinematic realm, as I don't think I've seen a single movie more than three times. (Or maybe there's something to be said for the need for novelty in its own right? Hmm...)

Anyway, gotta love a good deep dive into the psychology of strangers.

Have you seen any good movies lately?

STROLLER DADDY

*Children are a gift from the Lord;
they are a reward from Him.*
—Psalm 127:3

I've been asking the universe to help me project a more inviting and approachable vibe lately, and I swear it's been working. It seems like every other day, at least one new stranger is striking up a conversation with me, whereas before, I was definitely giving off a more aloof and closed-off vibe.

The other day, I went "surfing" (i.e., falling) on my lunch break, and on the way back to the car, a young man pushing a stroller stopped me to ask how long it took me to learn. I was honest and told him I'd just started, but here's a pro tip: The key to being a surfer is really just about *looking* like a surfer, carrying the board around with a swagger and strapping it to the roof of your car to look cool and whatnot. (Pay no attention to the huge rash on my chest because I didn't realize how much the wax can rub you raw.)

Anyway, this guy and I got to chatting and I asked him how fatherhood changed his life, to give me one positive and one negative thing. Immediately, he said, "The negative is you can't do whatever you want anymore. Someone's always gotta watch the baby." Then there was a pause and an exhale as he shook his head, mulling over the positive. I thought he was struggling to come up with a single one, but he put that notion to rest by saying, "There are too many positives to name."

That was encouraging to hear because I've at times wondered if I'd care to have children someday. Something about the freedom and financial cushion to be able to go out and do things like take up surfing on a whim sure is appealing. But when this guy took his child out of the stroller and let her wander over to the beach, and at the same time shared his positive, saying, "She's always so happy," she dug her toes into the sand and looked back at her father beaming with a smile and that moment seemed so priceless. Then he added, "Plus, chicks dig it," and I was sold.

Was there much wisdom to be derived from the above quote that you didn't already know? Probably not. But it's a good reminder that sometimes moments like these cross your path when you least expect it.

HOMELESS GAL

The Master said,
"Even when walking in the company of two other men,
I am bound to be able to learn from them.
The good points of the one I copy;
the bad points of the other I correct in myself."
—Analects of Confucius - Book 7, Chapter 22

I was eavesdropping on conversations on my stroll down the boardwalk this morning. Everything is out of context, so it's fun to plug in your own. Here, try:

"He just dropped off a huge duffle bag full of beer and left for Vietnam!"

I say Bruce Springsteen before they "sent me off to a foreign land to go and kill the yellow man."

"I don't wanna remember him like this, you know? I think I'm just gonna put him down."

After watching a kick of serial killer shows lately, my mind jumped to the assumption that she meant her husband.

The two people I'd like to focus on regarding the above quote, though, was a man who was on the telephone before the sun had even lit up the sky, yelling into the phone, saying, "He's drivin' me up a fuckin' wall!"

The juxtaposition between this guy and my conversation with the most attractive homeless gal I've ever seen shortly after was incredible.

(I'll pause to acknowledge the description of this latter person for a moment because I'm sure it stirred up some questions for you. Upon first approaching her, you never would have guessed it from the stylish outfit she was wearing. She surprised me with this fact soon into our conversation, and I was shocked. Anyway...)

Homeless Gal, despite her circumstances, had the utmost positive outlook on life and God. She had found herself in this situation after escaping a domestic violence situation and managed to keep a job as she floated around. I was floored by her optimism about how God must've made her homeless for a reason.

Meanwhile, Angry Phone Guy probably had a nice warm bed to wake up in every morning and a hot shower to go home to every night. Yet, before the day had even begun, he was all fired up with anger.

The contrast between these two people really put things into perspective because I've also woken up in a comfy bed, ready to burn down the world. From now on, anytime I'm even remotely close to that attitude, I plan to reflect on Homeless Gal and make sure I adopt her state of mind.

Thanks for the inspiration, HG.

BEACH PHILOSOPHER

*There is no greater sin than desire,
no greater curse than discontent,
no greater misfortune than wanting something for oneself.
Therefore, he who knows that enough is enough
will always have enough.
—Tao Te Ching - Verse 46*

I met a guy at the beach a while back, and we started talking about philosophy and religion. The next time I saw him, he told me, "I checked out your blog. I've seen most of those quotes before. They're all those things we're supposed to do but never apply."

I almost said, "Well, maybe *you* don't, pal!" But months later, I was half-reading this quote about desire, discontent, and wanting, while half-daydreaming about the things I desire, am discontented with, and want, and I flashed back to the beach and realized how true his words could be.

Not entirely true, and not all the time. I like to think some of the philosophizing I've done over the years has led to lasting change. But much of the wisdom disclosed in these ancient texts goes against the default settings wired into our brains.

When is enough ever enough? We always desire more; we are always discontent with the status quo; we always want novelty. The only times we don't is when we've been over-stimulated, over-satiated, and over-satisfied. And even then, it's just a protective mechanism that hits a temporary shut-off switch so we don't eat ourselves to death or what have you.

But I think the key is to keep reading these kinds of things as a constant reminder of what we're supposed to do, and hope that maybe that'll help you through the uphill trudge of applying them. Because what else is there to do except keep fighting the good fight? Give in to gluttony and indulgence?

I suppose. But where's the challenge in that?

So here's to you, Mister Random Beach Philosopher Guy. May you be doing the things that are most difficult to apply.

PSYCHO

The Master said,
"When we see men of worth,
we should think of equaling them.
When we see men of a contrary character,
we should turn inwards and examine ourselves."
—Analects of Confucius - 4:17

The other day, I saw a fifty-something year-old man take his shirt off at the beach. In the "tramp stamp" region of his back, there were letters tattooed that you could read from a mile away: **PSYCHO**.

This is a bold choice in life. Allow me to explain why.

As defined by the dictionary app on my phone, this word means, "An unstable and aggressive person," as in, "My ex is a total psycho."

Alternatively, UrbanDictionary.com offers, "A person who doesn't cry when Mufasa dies in *The Lion King*," which I think paints a sound picture of who we're dealing with here.

Let me just be clear: I'm not judging the application of permanent ink on your skin. In fact, I have a few tattoos myself. It was just this particular choice of word that caught me by surprise.

It wasn't long before he began approaching girls who were clearly several decades his junior, though, and I thought that perhaps the description fit the bill. And it was here that I began wondering what type of woman actually fancies a gentleman with such a label on his spine.

Perhaps those confused gals who kept writing Ted Bundy love letters in jail, for example. I mean, it's clearly a niche audience he had in mind when getting this permanent red flag. It's a serious filtration method that boils down the core group of options you have remaining—which, perhaps, is the point.

I just want to know if, before starting, the tattoo artist at least asked, "Are you *sure*?"

After I saw this man of contrary character get rejected by girls who weren't even born when *The Lion King* debuted, I decided to turn inward and examine myself.

I said, "Self, if you were to wear a giant noun as a tramp stamp on your back, what word would it be?"

I thought about "writer," or "humorist," or "philosopher," but they all sounded a tad arrogant when I imagined removing my shirt at the beach. And then a word popped into mind that stirs up as much intrigue as it does humble pity. A word that might draw someone in, instead of scare them away. A word that says, "I, too, cried when Mufasa died." And that word is **NERD**

What would your word be?

PULL-UPS AT CHURCH

*Do you not know that you are God's temple
and that God's Spirit dwells in you?*
—*1 Corinthians 3:1*

"This is my church," said the young man who'd joined me at the workout station by the shore. "I always have conversations like this at the pull-up bar."

It's true: You never know who you're gonna meet when you step outside your doorway. The beach has provided a number of friendships lately, but this one in particular took a quick and deep dive into biblical discussions.

One thing I've noticed since opening the Bible is the immediate communal bond with those seeking answers through the same text that has connected mankind for more than a thousand years.

Whether or not the things in that book are true, whether or not the text has been used to justify evil, whether or not it causes cultures to divide, there's something to be said about the connections it's spurred across space and time.

Friendships have been a theme coming up in meditations lately, and I've been asking God to send more of them my way. This felt like a prime example of "ask and you shall receive." I may never see that fella again, but it's a good reminder that some friendships last a lifetime, while others last the duration of a conversation. Either way, I'm grateful for all of them.

I never saw the pull-up bar as a "church" before, but I suppose any reason for people with similar interests to gather and strike up conversations about God could be considered a "church" of sorts. After all, it's the people who make up the church, not some empty building lined with candles and gold. The house of God is more like a tent we each carry on our backs that can be pitched anywhere we please.

So here's to you, random pull-up guy, and building churches, one rep at a time.

SHUT UP AND LISTEN

> *They enter into blind darkness*
> *who worship [ignorance and delusion];*
> *they fall, as it were, into greater darkness*
> *who worship [knowledge].*
> *The first leads to a life of action,*
> *the second to a life of meditation.*
> *But those who combine action with meditation*
> *cross the sea of death through action*
> *and enter into immortality through meditation.*
> *So have we heard from the wise.*
> *—Isa-Upanishad - Verse 9 -11*

The path of selfish pleasure without the pursuit of something higher is a dark one, but the path of acquiring knowledge for the sake of intellectual pride is even darker. Finding pleasure in the pursuit of knowledge applied with unselfish intentions is the most fulfilling path. At least, that's what I'm gathering.

I suppose immortality could refer to a clearer conscience and a purified soul connecting with the everlasting spirit of the universe, and the realization that you are one with the immortal God. But the practical application of this gem applies to this concept I've been adopting of trying to "be the light for others."

Last night, I was walking down the beach after a swim and came across a middle-aged woman sitting with her arms wrapped around her knees, looking troubled. I said hello, and she seemed receptive, so I asked what she was deep in thought about. It was amazing how quickly she opened up to a complete stranger about what was bothering her. (Then again, maybe it's easier to tell someone you'll never see again what's upsetting you than it is to tell someone who will remain in your life.)

I didn't even have to say anything; I just listened. At one point, I tried to offer insight, but she cut me off to keep talking, so I figured that was all she needed. I was only there for ten minutes before the sun was disappearing, and I told her I wanted to leave before it got dark. However, I could already see a shift in mood after a brief conversation with someone who stopped to genuinely listen.

Did I gain anything from hearing her woes? Not really. But to ease the pain in her eyes, even if just for a moment, felt worth the time. It cost me nothing, and all I had to do was listen, which is really nothing.

HELP

The Master said,
"The gentleman helps others to realize what is good in them.
He does not help them to realize what is bad in them.
The small man does the opposite."
—Analects of Confucius - Chapter 12, Verse 16

I believe there are people who genuinely want to help others, but I also believe there are folks who only want to help others because it makes them feel good about themselves. These are the kinds of people who will talk over you with unsolicited advice on a subject you didn't even realize you needed help with in the first place. What these people really need is a listener. In that case, listening to them help you is the most helpful thing you can do to help them.

But in doing so, aren't you just helping them because it makes you feel good about helping others? Which would make you no more helpful than they are, no?

This raises the question: Is listening politely really the most helpful thing you could do for these unhelpful helpers in the first place? Perhaps the most helpful thing would be to interrupt their helpfulness and tell them how unhelpful they really are.

But then, would your rudeness make you feel bad about helping others, therefore discouraging you from truly helping others at all? In which case, you'd be motivated to continue listening in an unhelpful manner because it's too painful to give them the help they actually need. This would mean you're acting purely out of self-interest, feeling better than you would if you acted helpfully because it would make you feel bad.

So, can you altruistically help others at all? And if so, how do you keep your helpfulness in check to a degree that it's not just a selfishly helpful act in itself?

Even if you could, wouldn't this mean that people who listen carefully and actually deliver relevant helpful advice are just a slyer version of the obviously selfish helpers? In which case, has my belief that there are people who are genuinely out there helping others now been disproven by my own attempt to help myself understand unhelpful people?

Please, help yourself by helping me with an answer in the comment section, you selfish bastard.

SELFISHLY SERVING OTHERS?

Charity given to a worthy person
simply because it is right to give,
without consideration of anything in return,
[...] is stated to be in the mode of goodness.
But charity given with reluctance,
with the hope of a return or in expectation of a reward,
is said to be in the mode of passion.
—*The Bhagavad Gita - Chapter 17, Verses 20-21*

I was in a recent discussion about serving others as a path to fulfillment, while remaining cautious that serving others isn't a distraction from addressing your own trauma.

Take, for example, a career in nursing: a noble profession on the surface, but underneath, it's a nonstop, high-stress environment where caring for others can take priority over caring for yourself. You have to ask yourself if choosing a career in caring for others can be a subconscious expression of the desire to be cared for.

Does, then, putting on the mask of Caretaker becomes a form of disingenuous service to others, as underneath, you've failed to care for yourself first?

Another way people serve others is by adopting pets, either consciously or subconsciously knowing that a fluffy friend will ease the pain of not feeling loved. Why face your fears and deal with trauma when you can simply plop a furball into your lap and experience the fleeting relief that comes with petting something soft and affectionate? As far as your neglected inner child is concerned, though, a furry distraction can be as much of a vice as filling the void with alcohol.

A third major path of distraction in serving others is by having children. Bringing a child into the world that will inherently love you is one way to fill the void. But as soon as those babies become independent teenagers and begin to separate themselves emotionally, that void filled with their dependency becomes empty again. That's because temporary dependency isn't a lasting solution to a persistent problem, just like pouring more water into a leaky bucket isn't a solution to maintaining a bucket full of water.

While these paths may appear to be therapeutic on the surface, it's important to realize that there are holes in your bucket that need to be patched up instead of constantly refilled. The point is, you owe it to yourself, your dog, your children, your significant other, or anyone else around you, to heal yourself so that you can become the best version of yourself in service to others.

UNRESOLVING CONFLICT

The Master said,
"The [superior man] acts in harmony with others
but does not seek to be like them.
The small man seeks to be like others
and does not act in harmony."
—Analects of Confucius - Chapter 13, Verse 23

Early in the improv class I'd signed up for, the teacher told us that whatever your partner tells you to do, you should do the opposite. For example, if I told you to take a seat in that chair, and you immediately sat down, then that's a boring resolution to the scene. But if you say, "No!" or maybe you question, "*That* chair?" then there's something to build off of. Maybe your character has an issue with authority, or they're a germaphobe, or who knows what, but the point is that there's a spark of intrigue to build off of why you wouldn't want to sit in that chair.

Our last scene on stage included "side coaching," where the teacher would pause us mid-scene and give tips and critique the performance. He stopped me multiple times in a row because every time my partner created conflict, I would immediately blurt out something that was conflict resolution, instead of resisting what was being said.

Multiple times in a row he had to stop me because apparently, this is how my brain is innately wired, and I couldn't seem to make the adjustment on the fly.

On the car ride home, I was trying to figure out why that was, and I realized this mentality was ingrained in me in childhood. I had a somewhat chaotic upbringing that involved walking on eggshells and dealing with random outbursts of conflict. Conflict resolution was the go-to safety mechanism to remedy whatever emotional outbursts I was dealing with, and that became my default response to conflict. But even today, it appears to be my go-to in the face of *fake* conflict, which is something that got exposed last night.

I'm not sure where the real-world application of this might appear later (perhaps in the workplace, friendships, or relationships), but it's good to know that the conscious beacon of light has begun illuminating this corner of darkness in the cave of the subconscious mind.

WINNING AN OSCAR

*"Now I will break their yoke from your
neck and tear your shackles away."*
—Nahum 1:13

Taking an improv class has been great for pushing emotional boundaries. Last night, our instructor spent the first ninety minutes of class evaluating our weaknesses and the last thirty minutes of class putting us in situations to exploit those weaknesses.

When my turn came, he pointed out that while I'm willing to walk to the edge of the emotional cliff, I seem unwilling to take the leap off. "I want you to jump off," he said.

A few minutes into my scene, he paused us to say, "I want you to look out over the class and into that 'camera' and deliver a monologue that's going to win you an Oscar."

I think the whole class could see how uncomfortable I was with the idea—being in the spotlight, expressing big emotions—but I played along.

For about thirty seconds anyway. Then, I tried to resume the scene.

"Do it again," he told me.

So I complied, bigger this time.

"And again," he said.

So I did, even bigger.

"*Again!*"

That's when I really jumped off, shouting passionately for my class and the "camera" to see.

I drove home feeling like I should throw my whole life away and move to L.A. to chase down a Hollywood dream.

I started reflecting on why it felt so good to leave it all on the table, and I realized it was because I grew up in a household where the over-expression of emotions was discouraged.

Quiet compliance was, well, encouraged in my home. So I learned to bottle up my feelings and operate on a pretty narrow emotional wavelength, to the point where expressing big emotions remained suppressed, even during an acting class. Being given permission to break through my usual calm and reservation was like being given the key to those restraints. Being forced to deliver an Oscar-winning monologue drove me over the precipice of emotional resistance.

PING PONG RESENTMENT

Knowing others is intelligence;
knowing yourself is true wisdom.
Mastering others is strength;
mastering yourself is true power.
—*Tao Te Ching - Verse 33*

Not to get all sci-fi on you, but I've been reflecting on triggering moments as if they're part of a simulation I signed up for—one *designed* to mirror childhood traumas. For example, I was in an improv class where the instructor frequently interrupted my scene with his "side coaching." I found myself becoming irritated because I felt he wasn't letting me be myself, and his constant interruptions were sucking the fun out of the scene.

After class, I reflected on why this might have triggered me, and the first memory that popped into my head was of learning to play ping pong with my father as a child. He was serving me a bucket of balls, and I was having a grand old time smacking them back over the net as hard as I could. That is, until he scolded me, saying, "Why don't you try and take this a *little* more seriously." Apparently, there was some minor resentment buried toward the authority figure raining on my parade, and a situation in which I felt I couldn't push back because of the power dynamic at play.

Apparently, this student/teacher dynamic here, where someone else was imposing their ideals onto my experience, resurrected those emotions to the point of feeling anger over something minor. But as soon as I was able to shine conscious awareness on the root of the unconscious reaction, those feelings pretty much disappeared.

Trying to examine situations like this as if they're a simulation playing out for you, as a means to mirror your past and trigger your emotions, allows you to take a step back from viewing them through an ego-protective lens and from seeing the other person as trying to offend you on purpose. This technique allows you to detach from the situation and evaluate it from an objective and less emotional perspective, so that you can dissolve the trigger at play.

DEFLECTING PRAISE

A solid rock by wind is undisturbed.
The wise by praise and blame are unperturbed.
—*The Dhammapada - Chapter 6, Verse 81*

"Perturbed" is an understatement for how being blamed makes me feel. The hair trigger on that reaction is better nowadays, but I'm still not quite the stoic I'd like to be in that department. No surprises there, but my natural response to praise, however, was an enlightening realization when it came to light. Instead of letting it go to my head to inflate my ego as you might expect, whenever I received a genuine compliment, I'd swat it aside with self-deprecating humor. I realized this, ironically enough, during a stand-up comedy class.

I happened to do particularly well performing a routine in progress and successfully made the class laugh. When I returned to my seat, the friend next to me laid her hand on my shoulder and sang my praises, saying, "Someday, I'll be able to look back and tell everyone that I knew you when you were just getting started." She, of course, meant this as an endearing compliment that implied my success, but I immediately quipped back with a tag-on, saying, "…and now he lives under the bridge downtown!" Which, of course, implied my own failure.

We both laughed, but as soon as we did, I realized I did this sort of thing with *all* genuine compliments thrown my way. It was a reflex to deflect them because, on a subconscious level, praise was unfamiliar, and therefore undeserved.

My reaction made me wonder how long I'd been doing that for. My whole life, it seemed, upon further reflection. I plan to publish the root experience in a more detailed book later on, so I won't dive into it all here, but the short of it is that my childhood brain had been wired to feel praise was foreign, so I'd dodge what felt undeserved in that way.

The lesson from The Dhammapada above is a simple and clear reminder not to be perturbed when faced with these kinds of stimuli, although possibly not in the way the quote was originally intended.

ARGUMENTS ARE A MIRROR

The wise man beholds all beings in the Self,
and the Self in all beings;
for that reason he does not hate anyone.
To the seer, all things have verily become the Self.
What delusion, what sorrow, can there be
for him who beholds that oneness?
—Isa-Upanishad - Verses 6-7

I recently got into a minor argument with someone, and in the heat of the moment, I could recognize how our frustrations mirrored one another. Each of us saw the other as stubborn in our way, and the discussion was going in circles. I don't like interactions like this, but they're important for reflecting on traits about oneself, or perhaps repeating stories from childhood. In this one, I could feel a trigger from a parental relationship bubbling up from adolescence. Fortunately, in this case, this person and I could agree to disagree and end the conversation with respect. It was not so much the case back then.

Anyway, I've scratched the surface of reading stoic philosophy over the years, and I believe in the importance of being in control of your emotions, but there are still times when I allow mine to get the best of me. Whenever this occurs, I immediately try to dig into why it happened and resolve the underlying issue that lingers beneath the surface. This practice has allowed me to mature from the state of a leaf in the wind toward that of an immovable stone. I'm not quite there yet, but it's the recognition when it happens and the ability to reflect upon it that's important.

I've seen this concept of others providing a mirror for what you love and hate in yourself floating around as new age internet memes, but here we can see the concept dates back thousands of years. We should strive to be this seer of self in others and others in self, and hope to one day be the wise man who feels no anger, no sorrow, no delusion. The realization of oneness melts away the sense of diversity and, therefore, the cause of misery along with it. Or, as Eknath Easwaran translates the last line above, "How can the multiplicity of life delude the one who sees its unity?"

FLIGHT PRAYERS

*Seek help through patience and prayers.
God helps those who endure in hard times.
—The Qur'an - 2:153*

I hate waiting in lines. (I say this merely to distinguish myself from those who love waiting in lines.) However, they do give you time to think.

I was thinking about how last night as I set my alarm for 3:30 a.m. to catch an early flight, I was putting positive thoughts out to the universe for a smooth journey. However, upon my arrival at the airport, I discovered that my flight had been canceled while I was stumbling out the door like a zombie…

So, in line for flight reassignment, I was wondering why people pray for outcomes that are ultimately out of their control. Is it to make ourselves feel some semblance of control over our lives? To reach for optimism in the face of pessimism? To hope for order in a world full of chaos? If there is a God, do we think one of a billion prayers coming in daily will influence His grand plan?

As hard as we pray for smooth travels, prosperity, or good health, can you really pray your way out of canceled flights, financial woes, or even cancer if they're in the cards? Is this behavior just reinforcing a desire for control over things that are out of our control when we could, instead, adopt the more practical approach of some of the Eastern religions in letting go of attachment to outcomes?

Is there a purpose in praying for things at all, or should we focus on being grateful for whatever comes our way while walking the path before us with grace? If there is an omniscient God, doesn't He already knows what we want? So do we really need to beg for it? Or does articulating our desires in the form of prayer fall under the "ask and you shall receive" umbrella? Does God want us to voice the desires He already knows we have as a form of humbling action? But then again, He doesn't always deliver on what we want, now does He?

I'm afraid I have more questions than answers for you today, but sometimes that's just how it goes.

FLOWING TO THE DENTIST

The highest good is like water.
Water gives life to ten thousand things and doesn't strive.
It flows in places men reject and so is like the Tao.
        —*Tao Te Ching - Verse 8*

"May I help you?"

This is how the short-tempered receptionist at the nearest dental office answered the phone when I called to set up an appointment. When I asked how she was doing today, there was a pause and a sigh before she more impatiently said, "*May I help you?*"

When I asked how soon I could get in, she told me she could pencil me in in about three months. "Let me get back to you." Click.

I called a second office, less conveniently located twenty minutes away. An angel was the receptionist there. They could even see me today.

During pleasant conversation amidst hooks being jabbed into my gums, the hygienist told me she'd read the entire Bible on her own by the age of fourteen. Hashtag motivating (although I question how much rape, incest, murder, and deceit a young gal should be exposed to).

Upon final inspection, the doctor said, "Boy, you're a boring patient. Nancy, can you write this guy a script to start abusing more candy so we can get some real work out of him?"

He also had a killer mustache. I doubt the doctor at the first office had a killer mustache.

At first, I questioned why the more convenient location couldn't see me sooner. From this, I learned that the most convenient option may not always be the best option.

Note to self: Stop questioning the universe and flow with life like water.

LET GO OF THE STEERING WHEEL

Let go of the past, let go of the future, let go of the present, and cross over to the farther shore of existence.
—The Dhammapada - Chapter 24, Verse 348

I was talking to a friend about plans for the future. He mentioned his son, who's in the military with the next twenty-five years of his career mapped out. I'm in a branch of sales where if I knew this was the next twenty-five years of my life, I might go insane. As much as the unknown is intimidating, I think I need a bit of mystery in my future just to keep me on my toes.

A while back, I decided to let go of the steering wheel of life and trust in the way things will unfold. I did this because none of the ideas I had about the future ever played out as I had envisioned. You meet a person, and your life takes a left instead of the right you foresaw. An opportunity arises, and you take a right instead of the left you had planned.

If you had told me a year ago that I'd be studying religious scriptures, I would have said you were crazy.

If you had told me five years ago that I'd move back to Florida, I would have said, "Not a chance."

If you had told me ten years ago that I'd spend a year of my life in Saudi Arabia, I would have said, "Where?"

None of these things were on my radar; they just emerged from the fog before me, and I rolled with them.

Since no one can see what's coming, my philosophy is now something more like, "Why invest so much energy in mapping out a future that's ultimately out of our control?"

While others may have more stability in the bedrock of their lives, that element of surprise can strike anyone at any time and shake things up to a jarring degree. I believe it's healthy to always maintain a sense of non-attachment when it comes to your idea of what's to come.

JEFFREY DAHMER 1

*They who see themselves in all
and all in them
help others through spiritual osmosis
to realize the Self themselves.*
—*Katha Upanishad - Part 2, Verse 8*

Man, I've been watching this Jeffrey Dahmer docuseries on Netflix. Talk about practicing this "seeing yourself in others and others in yourself" crap. Now *that* pushes the limits of sympathy right there.

I will say, though, they've done a wonderful job of dramatizing the impact on everyone involved. There was this touching father-son moment after Dad found out his little Jeffy was eating people, and boy, a part of you starts to go, "Aww. Isn't that swee—" Then there's a pause as you wonder if you should really be feeling that way toward a monster. So now I'm just over here reflecting on all these lessons on love and compassion, trying to put myself in Dahmer's shoes and debating whether or not there should be room for any of that.

(Speaking of room, the *Hannibal* series was another recent favorite of mine. You're lying to yourself if Chef Mads Mikkelsen didn't make you at least a teensy bit curious about trying a good leg steak. Did you see all those fresh ingredients??

"Find out if I dabble in cannibalism next time on *The Devout Humorist*!")

Jokes aside, trying to put yourself inside the mind of a cannibalistic serial killer is a darkeningly enlightening exercise. After pushing those boundaries, it's much easier to sympathize with that person you bump heads with at work or that guy who was rude in line at the bank. It's much easier to brush it off and assume they're having a bad day if there's not a legitimate fear they might chop you up into bits and eat your liver.

Let's bring it back to what may be my new favorite term, "spiritual osmosis," and use this exercise to help others realize the Self by seeing ourselves in others first.

JEFFREY DAHMER 2

"We deserve to die for our crimes,
but this man hasn't done anything wrong."
Then he said, "Jesus, remember me
when you come into your Kingdom."
And Jesus replied, "I assure you, today
you will be with me in paradise."
—Luke 23:41-43

Jeffrey Dahmer was an inspiration. (To some, that is. Not me in particular.) But Dahmer was also inspired, by the likes of John Wayne Gacy, although for a different reason than you're probably thinking.

Jesus.

Yes, a man who raped and strangled 33 young men was the inspiration for a man who killed and ate 17 young men in finding the Lord.

Weird.

(Spoiler alert for the docuseries ending.)

The dramatization shows Gacy on television discussing the artwork he'd been working on while on death row, designed to "bring joy into people's lives," when he mentioned being at peace with everything he'd done because of his relationship with God. This sparked Dahmer's curiosity in finding the Lord.

Initially doubtful that he could ever be forgiven, the biblical scene above was the one revealed to Dahmer by the prison reverend, giving him hope. It was explained that of the two criminals crucified alongside Christ, after the first one mocked the Messiah, the second one acknowledged him as the Son of God, and that's all it took to secure a place alongside him in the Kingdom of Heaven.

Apparently, Gacy was executed on the same day Dahmer was baptized, on the same day of a solar eclipse.

Weird.

The following scene depicts Dahmer's neighbor, who tried and failed numerous times to get the police to investigate the abnormal sounds and smells emerging from her neighbor's apartment. She was speaking to the pastor of her own church, struggling to find any forgiveness in her heart for the man who disturbed her life in numerous ways.

This sparks my question for today's post: Could *you* forgive Jeffrey Dahmer?

And if you were one of the victim's parents, Could you forgive the man who ate your son?

That's a heavy question to weigh.

After being baptized, the pastor tells Dahmer, "Congratulations, Jeff. You're saved."

If that's the case, eternity seems like a long time to spend in the company of Dahmer and Gacy...

#SeeYouBoysInHeaven

#MullThatOver

THE UNABOMBER

*Through compassion,
the naked hermit reflects upon his inner self.
He slays his own self, instead of slaying others.
—Siri Guru Granth - Ang 356*

I'm on a streak of watching serial killer shows—*Mind Hunters*, *Sons of Sam*, *The Unabomber*—and I'm fascinated by the psychology behind why these people did what they did. The more I study trauma healing, the more I heal my own past, the more I can see how extreme environments create psychopaths, and—dare I say—even find some compassion for them.

I can't help but wonder, if I were exposed to the same conditions, could I have turned my life around? It's easy to ride your high horse of ethics and morals now, but to dissolve your own reality and question what would really happen is another story.

Surely there are paths to choose in life, and no one is excusing their behaviors, but can society admit that it's partially responsible for churning out such monsters?

The Unabomber is a perfect example—born a happy baby until he fell ill in his first year of life, where he was hospitalized for months, left almost completely alone because the doctors wouldn't allow his parents to visit more than twice a week. After that, he was never the same.

What kind of abandonment issues does that imprint on a child at their most impressionable age? The kind that drives a man to become an ice-cold killer hellbent on tearing down a society?

Without the backstory, you see an evil man set on creating chaos, but examine the details and you find a resentful child motivated by pain.

Was there any path to healing such trauma? Would regular therapy have even worked? Could, perhaps, the psychedelic treatments we see healing trauma today have reversed his past, were it not deemed illegal before he set off the first bomb?

You have to ask: Did Ted Kaczynski terrorize the system, or did the system terrorize Ted?

Where am I going with this, you wonder? Me too.

Perhaps it's an exercise in the deepest form of compassion.

Perhaps it's a promotion for the legality of psychedelic therapy.

Perhaps it's just a subtle advertisement for various Netflix films.

The world may never know. All you can do is pop yourself a bowl of popcorn and observe.

WESTERN NOSTALGIA

We are human beings of the briefest moment.
We do not know the appointed time of our departure.
—Siri Guru Granth - Ang 660

I was watching this Netflix series called *Godless* last night, which shows a glimpse into the Old Western era. There's something appealing about that time in history, when the world was wild and lawless. Life could be just a man and his horse, exploring unexplored countryside, drinking water from streams and living off the land. It was a simpler existence, when your concerns were mostly about survival, when disputes were settled by gunfire, when death was on the forefront of the mind at all times.

That mindset seems lost today, drowned out by login passwords and social media feeds.

How many hours have we spent at the DMV while our ancestors were riding horseback through mountains?

How much time is spent swiping through apps instead of navigating land by stars?

How many days are spent saving for retirement while our brethren roamed wastelands to stake out the land they'd die on?

What a different life that must have been—more intense, more alive. Sometimes I wonder if I was born in the wrong era.

Of course, I could probably figure out how to live somewhat like that, even today. Move out west to some off-grid ranch and learn to mosey around on horseback and whatnot.

Could I hack it? Would I miss the WiFi? Or would I be so present and preoccupied that it wouldn't even cross my mind, aware that death may lurk around any corner in the wild? (At least a degree closer to what our predecessors felt, anyway.)

As Frank Griffin from *Godless* said, "The same God that made you and me also made the rattlesnake." Something about that sounds like a more fitting way to go, as opposed to getting hit by a city bus or rotting away in some hospital bed. Maybe someday they'll find my remains plucked apart by desert wildlife, but for now, my reality remains in the age of the internet, with the concept of death buried somewhere beneath potential material buys and search engine optimization.

ARE YOU DEAD INSIDE?

The wise who know the Self,
bodiless,
seated within perishable bodies,
great and all-pervading,
grieve not.
—Katha Upanishad - Part 2, Verse 22

I started watching a documentary called *The Alpinist* about a guy who's been ascending his way up history's boldest climbers list. The fella spent most of his "career" dead broke, living in a stairwell, doing nothing but enjoying a free-spirited lifestyle.

As someone who's afraid of heights, I barely had the courage to watch, never mind considering getting out there. But it led me to wonder how many of us partake in any activities in our lifetimes where a single false move could mean our demise. Other than driving, I suppose, but that doesn't come with the zeroed-in bliss described by Marc-André Leclerc while he solos snowy, icy, rocky peaks that other climbers wouldn't even dare. He puts his life on the line on a daily basis, just for kicks.

I don't get the impression Marc is a Hindu sage, but he seems to have found his way toward realizing the body and Self are separate entities. Diagnosed with ADHD as a square child forced into a round public school system, he found a hobby that cleared his "squirrel mind," as he called it. Ascending deadly cliffs became his way to achieve inner silence.

After a climb that had him dangling off a cliff by one arm, an interviewer asked, "How was it?"

Marc's reply was, "Super fun!"

"Scary?"

"Not really."

"Are you dead inside?" I hoped the interviewer might ask. Or has he realized such a level of non-attachment that fear no longer exists?

But where is the line between foolish and brave, bold and stupid, free and insane? This is what I wondered as I shoveled more pre-popped popcorn into my face on a comfy couch. I'm not even sure if those questions were answered because I turned in like a good little cog in the wheel to be well-rested for my 9-5 the next day.

I don't think we should all abandon society to live in stairwells, but there is something to be admired about such a free spirit, and perhaps a lesson to be had about not fearing mortality that we can apply to our own lives.

Although that said, Marc did mention dropping six tabs of acid at a party once, so maybe all this can be chalked up to a fried circuit.

LEWIS & CLARK

*When I consider Your heavens, the work of Your fingers,
the moon and the stars, which You have set in place,
what is mankind that You are mindful of them,
human beings that You care for them?*
—*Psalms 8:3-4*

"How could you have lost your fire starter!?" I yelled at the contestant on the TV show *Alone*. "Don't you realize that fire is *everything*?" I reclined into the comfort of my chair and forked another gluttonous mouthful of lunch down my throat. "You moron," I said, spewing food particles as I watched him cope with the delirium of starvation. I have no experience surviving in the wilderness myself, of course, but you know how easy it is to quarterback from a recliner.

I did go backcountry camping in a national park once. A friend and I lugged gallons of water up a well-worn trail to the top of Yosemite just to find out there was snow we could have melted all along. We ate satisfactory meals and were hindered by a weak cell phone signal, struggling through a single night at the very edge of civilization.

This near Lewis and Clark experience will stick with me forever, though, because it was the first time I slept under the stars, as we opted not to pitch the tent that night. And when I say "stars," I mean you could see the whole Milky Way Galaxy, clear as anything published in *National Geographic*, complete with meteors streaking across the tapestry of constellations twinkling along the skyline. The only thing missing was a David Attenborough voiceover sharing valuable tidbits of information.

I recall being snuggly tucked within a circle of rocks forming a wall around me near the cliff's edge while my friend chose a more open space further from the precipice.

"Be careful," he called out, mocking me just before bed. "Try not to roll off the edge!"

"You too," I replied. "This close to winter, I hear the bears are hungry!"

There was a strong silence.

"Night," I added, rolling over noisily.

"You're a real piece of shit," I heard a weaker voice say.

If there's one thing I learned from that trip, it's that the vulnerability of sleeping cliffside in black bear country is worth the unobscured glimpse into eternity that's otherwise blocked by light pollution. Will I ever brave the Alaskan frontier in grizzly country while depending on a fire starter for survival? Perhaps not. But that small taste of wilderness sure has awoken something in me that craves more.

HAKUNA MATATA

*When something seems too easy,
difficulty is hiding in the details.
—Tao Te Ching - Verse 63*

I used to be pretty dead behind the eyes when it came to watching movies, but somewhere along the line of healing, I've become far more in tune with my "feelings." For example, I recently watched *The Lion King* for the first time since childhood. I wasn't expecting a cartoon with happy sing-along songs to touch me, but between Mufasa's death, the "Can you feel the love tonight?" scene, and Simba's redemption arc, I found some of those pesky little emotions bubbling up to the surface.

Sappy stuff aside, one thing that stuck out was the "Hakuna Matata" phase Simba went through. This two-word, problem-free philosophy was purported to solve all your problems. It emptied life of worries and filled it with eating and swimming in paradise. But while that catchy little tune has you singing along so happily, underneath was nothing but the hedonistic escape from a painful past. Living a life of impulsive pleasures and doing whatever you want can be appealing for a while, but that youthful phase can only last so long.

Fortunately, Nala appears, with her allure of an ideal love that awakens Simba to his higher calling, humbling him with resentment toward the avoidant outcast he's become while hanging out with his dopey pals.

As Simba begins reaching for the dangling carrot that will eventually lead him toward living up to his potential, Timon and Pumbaa sing a duet that says, "If he falls in love tonight, it can be assumed… his carefree days with us are history. In short, our pal is doomed." Yeah, doomed to take on moral responsibilities and fulfill his destiny, sung from the viewpoint of two bums who just sit around and eat grub all day. (How 'bout takin' a hike, you worthless warthog and miserable meerkat! Simba's got bigger things to do.)

I'm all about giving credit where it's due, so let's just sum this little reflection up by pointing out the true champion of our story: Without Nala, the low-key heroine that drew the lion king out of his self-indulgent slumber, Scar would still be ruling over Pride Rock today.

#LongLiveTheQueen

GARDEN PARALLEL

*"Put your sword back into its place,
for all who draw the sword will die by the sword."*
—Matthew 26:52

I thought of a metaphorical parallel between the biblical summary and a potential parent-child relationship arc. God—or the parental figure the child sees as an all-powerful symbol of creation—brings you into existence whether you asked for it or not. The Garden of Eden—or the psychological blank slate with which you enter the world—is initially a paradise-like existence where there is nothing to worry about, as all of your needs are taken care of.

But there are rules in this world—like "Don't eat from that tree," or maybe "Don't steal cookies from the cookie jar." If you violate these rules—even out of curiosity, succumbing to the temptation of that (serpent-like) voice whispering in your ear—there is reprimand and punishment. Being scolded by your creator makes you feel ashamed, disappointing the one who made you and opening your eyes to the fact that there are both good and evil ways to behave in this world.

But if you hold onto that shame and guilt, you may also harbor resentment and anger toward the parental figure who made you feel those things. At that point, the spirit of negativity will accompany you as you leave home and find your own way in the world. At some point in life, though, a Christ-like spirit may enter your life and reveal how holding onto negativity isn't good for your own well-being and should, therefore, be cast out.

But—in the same way that Christ didn't defeat the oppressive Rome—you must acknowledge that you can't change the world around you. However, you can change your reaction to the world around you by accepting the way things are—just like Christ didn't resist the Romans who took him captive for prosecution.

Therefore, the ego—a protective mechanism that came about in reaction to the parental figure—must be sacrificed on the metaphorical cross. That is the liberating path back to the Heaven-like state in which you were born.

By addressing the root of trauma, casting out the spirit of negative emotions, and sacrificing the ego, forgiving and honoring your parents becomes the key to your own salvation and return to the blissful existence in which you entered the world.

HORSE-AND-BUGGY

"The truth will set you free."
—John 8:32

I recently attended a church service with a couple of friends, and we went to a diner afterward. Over French toast and egg sandwiches, we discussed the vast array of different churches, preachers, and attendees that have spanned over time.

The churches I've attended sporadically over the years were more old school—with robes and candles—while these friends are members of something more new age—with live bands and a video production crew. My friend's wife was raised in a cult-like setting that called these new-age churches evil, yet attendance in these newer environments is growing, while attendance in older churches is dying off (literally).

"Maybe they are," said my friend, "but even if they do, they served their purpose to get us where we are today."

They were the horse-and-buggy to today's automotive, I suppose. But the evolution of the delivery of the message is interesting. The old-school vibe I experienced seemed more piecemeal, with lots of hymns and random snippets of verses here and there, which weren't as cohesive as the man in a suit jacket delivering a modern sermon here.

Our discussion drifted toward how each pastor, reverend, or minister can interpret the roughly 1,700 pages of biblical text however they want. And, being a vast spectrum of deliverers—ranging from good to evil and everything in between—that text can pretty much say whatever they want it to say by pasting different verses together and creating correlations. And then there are the deliverees—ranging from ignorant and impressionable to well-versed and informed—who can pretty much absorb whatever they want with a filter of their own selective hearing. So God's Word—the "Truth," if you will—is shaped and understood differently by man, intentionally or unintentionally, depending on who is doing the interpreting.

Our conclusion was that responsibility comes down to the individual to study and learn for themselves—something the minority take the initiative to do—otherwise, you're at the mercy of whoever is at the head of the church, receiving a grab bag approach to religion. That's the real truth.

RELIGIOUS BAGGAGE

Do not be deceived:
Bad company corrupts good morals.
—1 Corinthians 15:33

The label "religion" often carries baggage; therefore, the texts of each religion bear the weight of humanity's actions that have snowballed over time, well after these ancient stories were actually written down. I think the primary reason it took me so long to crack open these books was the stigma surrounding "religion," even though I had little grasp of what each text actually said.

If these stories were separated from the Biblical canon, for example, and stood alone on a bookshelf labeled "Humanities Myths & Origin Stories," I might have picked them up sooner. If the back sleeve of a book called *Genesis* read something like, "Follow mankind's evolution through ancient Israel's origin story. From the time a great deity molded man out of clay and breathed life into his lungs, to a brother sold into slavery who rises up to become the governor of Egypt, this riveting series of tales tracks early humans through the trials and tribulations of founding civilization in the cradle of life," that might have piqued my interest while browsing through bookstores for Joseph Campbell-type literature.

I was completely taken aback by what I found in the first book of the Bible. I had no idea it was filled with stories of rape, incest, murder, and betrayal. I had no idea what to expect, but it sure wasn't a bunch of tales of lies, deceit, and chaos.

Imagine perusing another bookshelf labeled "Most Popular Short Stories of All Time" and reading a summary of Job that says, "Explore one of literature's most confounding mysteries in a tale that explores why bad things happen to good people. Witness an innocent man endure the worst of tragedies, one after another, all to settle a wager between Satan and God." Would you be more intrigued if you didn't have to flip through much of a leather-bound Bible to get there? If so, I'd encourage anyone to put aside the labels of "religion" and just read these stories as best sellers passed down throughout the generations.

SOME THINGS SHOULD NEVER CHANGE

Suppose a man marries a woman,
but after sleeping with her, he turns against her
and publicly accuses her of shameful conduct, saying,
"When I married this woman,
I discovered she was not a virgin."
[...] The men of the town must stone her to death.
—Deuteronomy 22:13-21

It was tough to find applicable wisdom for today's world in Deuteronomy, but reading it made me wonder why we throw out a huge percentage of the rules God supposedly laid out for us, while choosing to hold onto others—particularly in the realm of sexuality, which still seems to be stigmatized by the church and society.

Do you still put women apart for seven days because her "issue in her flesh be blood"?

Do you think if your son doesn't listen to his parents, he should be stoned to death?

Do you think if a priest's daughter defiles herself with promiscuity, she should be burned alive?

Do you believe a crippled man or a hunchback or a dwarf has no right to approach the altar of God because he's defected?

No? Then why do you hold onto guilt around sexual stigmas tied to the Bible?

Some of these rules might get God canceled on Twitter, for Pete's sake, so who arbitrarily picks which ones stay and which ones go? I must've missed the voting ballot.

If, for example, two consenting adults wish to open their marriage to include others, should this be condemned under the banner of "adultery"? Meanwhile, the morals regarding slave ownership and rules for stoning others sandwich this one.

If whoever has the answer to these questions could please dial in to the show and explain it to us, [*Office Space* voice] "That'd be great."

(Please enjoy this complimentary ad for ChristianSwingers.com while your party is reached.)

Maybe the lesson here is that change is the only constant, and no one should have the authority to choose which rules are relevant today and which are as archaic as the times they were written. Except for that one about putting women to death if you find out they aren't virgins. Obviously, some things should never change.

DONKEY > MARY

Then the Lord opened the mouth of the donkey,
and she said to Balaam,
"What have I done to you,
that you have struck me these three times?"
And Balaam said to the donkey,
"Because you have made a fool of me.
I wish I had a sword in my hand,
for then I would kill you!"
—Numbers 22:28-29

I could never understand how this Judeo-Christian story is defended as literal truth, but that's fine. It's also a story thrown out by critics when I knew there was still value to be derived, so I didn't want to do that either. I don't associate myself with any religion, so I don't have to worry about defending whether it's literal truth or not. Instead, I can view it along the lines of one of Aesop's fables.

(I will say, though, the most unbelievable part isn't that a donkey spoke, but that the man who owned the donkey didn't even bat an eyelash when it started talking!)

Anyway, Balaam was on his way to do something the Lord was unhappy with, so the Lord sent an angel to stand in his path. Balaam, blinded by his intentions, failed to see the angel that his donkey noticed. As the angel drew his sword, the donkey turned off the path. Balaam, still oblivious, beat his donkey for veering off course. Twice more similar events occurred before we see the quote above. Then the Lord opened the eyes of Balaam so that he saw the angel before him with its sword drawn. He fell to his knees as the angel told him it may have killed him if not for his donkey.

I'll leave the debate over whether a donkey spoke or whether it was an auditory illusion aside. These matters of "right" and "wrong" are beside the lessons we can derive here.

Lesson #1: When blinded by poor motivation, we may think the actions of faithful friends are against us when really they have our best intentions in mind.

Lesson #2: Who at first appears to be a sword-drawn adversary in our way may really be the voice of reason stopping the progress of our evil ways.

Lesson #3: Sometimes, it takes nothing short of a miracle for the inaudible to become audible and the invisible to become visible.

Just as my own first impression was to throw this story out as nonsense, there was more to it than initially seen.

(Bonus Fun Fact: There are more biblical words dedicated to this talking ass than the mother of Jesus! Imagine that.)

BELL CURVE

*"My command is this:
Love each other as I have loved you."*
—John 15:12

I've started perusing different religion subreddits and came across this post on r/Christianity:

"I've been a Christian for five years but have only recently talked to other Christians. I now understand why so many people hate Christianity because Christians are some of the rudest, hypocritical, hateful assholes I have ever met. So many just call themselves Christian but don't follow a single Christian value. I will always be Christian, but this community is terrible and I hate being associated with a lot of these people."

My first thought was that there are 2+ billion Christians, so there's inevitably a bell curve of assholes on one end, saints on the other, and the majority of people somewhere in between. But the command laid out by Jesus above may seem impossible to live up to in the face of rude, hypocritical, and hateful assholes (especially when the "as I have loved you" meant willingness to go to the cross), but I think we can strive to do our best when dealing with these types.

While that might not be genuinely manifesting those warm and fuzzy feelings associated with love, we at least have it within our power to act lovingly toward each other, even if others don't reciprocate the same attitude. Pouring more rudeness or hatred into the world doesn't do anyone any good. Also, we have it in our power to cultivate and strengthen our emotions by focusing on the attitude that is favorable or unfavorable toward someone else, by seeking out what is lovable or unlovable in others, despite whether or not they are more narrow-minded, despite whether or not their worldview is entirely different from ours.

When it comes to following this command, I think our role is to uphold our own standards and echo the nature of Christ's love the best we can.

APHRODITE

You shall have no other gods before Me.
—Exodus 20:3

In Exodus 20:3, Yahweh states, "You shall have no other gods before Me." Your first reaction may be a double-take, asking yourself if God just acknowledged the existence of other gods.

Were these other deities that existed unrelated to, but on a similar plane as, the Judeo-Christian Creator? Were these the supposed angels, like Satan, who rebelled against Yahweh?

One interpretation could take into account the mythological manifestation of certain innate human traits—like Venus or Aphrodite, for example: the embodiment of love, lust, and sexual desire from Greco-Roman mythology.

If what is meant is that you shall not allow the grip of sexual desire to rule over you in a way that interferes with your focus on the Most High, then this is an interpretation I can relate to. Though I have this inner guiding compass that steers me away from promiscuity, there is also a rather loud voice extending from the loins that urges me to indulge in that venture. Although I follow the higher compass (winning the overall war), that lower voice often seems to steer the ship astray in the day-to-day (winning smaller battles). Chatting up those I find attractive in public, for example, or spending time messaging interests through text or social media, or expending energy indulging in fantasy, all fall into this category. Although none of these things are a complete cave-in to promiscuity, the goddess of lust still has a grip that outweighs my focus on my higher calling at times.

That goddess could be any number of things for anyone—like gluttony, greed, anger, or the urge to drink—but none should have a grip so hard that they detract your attention from where your focus should be. Allowing yourself to succumb to the temptation of whatever other "god" you might worship is a diffusion of energy that could otherwise be put toward the higher purpose God is calling you toward.

This, I believe, is a modernly relevant interpretation of Yahweh's, "Have no other gods before Me."

MAD MINUTE

*One who seeks knowledge
learns something new every day.
One who seeks the Tao
unlearns something new every day.*
—*Tao Te Ching - Verse 47*

Math was never my strong suit. I can remember in third grade being regularly outperformed in the "Mad Minute"—a sixty-second blitz to mentally calculate as many multiplication problems as possible. In high school, I remember the pressure of being called on in pre-calc and my brain being about as useful as a bowl of Jell-O.

Last night, I woke up to a dream of a similar grade school embarrassment and realized the fear of public shame has fueled my pursuit of knowledge above all else. Every opportunity I get, from the time I wake to the time I sleep, is filled with reading or listening to something educational. And if I'm not doing something to expand my knowledge base, I get anxious that I'm wasting time. Even the pursuit of meditation (and my relationship with God, to some degree) has come second to the pursuit of knowledge. Here, I recognized the parallel of "putting no other God before Me" as discussed in a recent post about chasing Aphrodite and the temptation of lust.

Sometimes, I think I get woken up in the middle of the night with trauma-healing insights or good ideas because that's the only time my mind is quiet enough to receive them. In the sense that the smart man learns something every day while the wise man unlearns something every day, I'm so busy spending my conscious hours pursuing knowledge that I give myself no space to receive wisdom.

Learning as much as possible all the time has been driven by a grade school fear of classmates finding out I'm dumb because I wasn't very good at math. But as I dissolved this trauma, I realized that in the end, the last laugh is mine because my only Mad Minute limitation now is how fast my fingers can type into the calculator app on my phone. Take *that*, Mrs. Third Grade Teacher Whose Name Has Been Forgotten.

GHOSTS OF THE PAST

*"And so I tell you,
every kind of sin and slander can be forgiven,
but blasphemy against the Spirit will not be forgiven."*
—Matthew 12:31

I was having a conversation with someone last night who dislikes the boy's character in my book, *Genesis: Biblical Commentary Through Dialogue*. She grew up in a Catholic school system and was on the receiving end of guilt, shame, and scolding if she questioned the "authority figures" in the system. She told me the boy made her uncomfortable asking all of his questions, and I correctly guessed that was her inner child's lingering fear of getting in trouble bubbling up to the surface whenever the boy asked something she herself had but was afraid to ask because of this trauma. I told her there was an inner dichotomy between wanting to ask the questions herself and her younger self wanting to punch the boy in the arm and say, "Shh! You're gonna get us in trouble!" Obviously, there is no authority figure to get her in trouble today, but the traumatized younger version of herself still living inside her doesn't realize that.

This, of course, was the purpose of the boy's character all along, while the purpose of the old man is to represent someone confident enough in his faith to patiently answer these questions where a "traditional" (and potentially less confident) authority figure might respond with guilt or shame and no answers. The whole purpose of the book is to allow the reader permission to ask the challenging questions they may feel like they don't have the permission to ask and *not* be faced with shame and guilt, but instead find the appropriate answers delivered in a patient manner.

Now, if only the reviewer on Amazon who gave my book one star for "blasphemy" could see things that way.

FOR ARGUMENT'S SAKE

> *"One is the road that leads to wealth,*
> *another the road that leads to Nirvana."*
> *If [...] the disciple of Buddha has learnt this,*
> *he will not yearn for honor,*
> *he will strive after separation from the world.*
> —The Dhammapada - Chapter 5, Verse 75

Growing up, I was often faced with an impenetrable wall of irrationality. That created stories in my subconscious that have plagued me ever since. One of those stories came to light yesterday.

I was dealing with the provider of a service I needed, outlining a case for how they failed to meet the expectations that were advertised. In a court of law, all the necessary evidence to win the case was there. But we weren't in a court of law. In reality, this person had my money and refused to see eye-to-eye with me despite their satisfaction guarantee.

I spent a lot of time digging into our written exchanges and highlighting every instance where it appeared the provider was wrong and even suggested a couple of potentially fair compromises. But I was met with nothing but downplaying, denying, or refusing to acknowledge the evidence that was in front of them, and a resolution could only have come from convincing them to see things rationally, which could not be done.

That drove me crazy.

After a while, it wasn't even about the money. The story I found myself living out again was, "I just want you to acknowledge that you're wrong." When I realized this, just the act of labeling the story offered a sense of relief, as I'd now shone a spotlight on another dark corner of the unconscious mind, which was probably worth the money in itself.

In doing so, I also recognized how the desire to penetrate the impenetrable wall became the driving force behind my becoming a good communicator, which is a good skill to have. My unconscious motivation was that if I could just express myself in a way that makes enough sense, then I can get the other person to see my point of view. (Honestly, I may have missed a path in life toward becoming a defense lawyer because I can't help but to spend extensive periods of time laying out detailed arguments in the name of injustice).

Repeatedly living out subconscious stories within your lifetime is, in a sense, living out reincarnations of Hell cycles in different phases. But free yourself from the subconscious stories, and you'll steer your mind toward a state of Nirvana.

PRODUCTIVITY IS THE DEVIL

Fill your bowl to the brim and it will spill.
Keep sharpening your knife and it will blunt.
Chase after money and your heart will never unclench.
Care about people's approval and you will be their prisoner.
—*Tao Te Ching - Verse 9*

I've taken time off from writing posts to work on a manuscript I'm finishing, and there was a twinge of guilt about not posting here during that time. Of course, the whole thing was in my head because there's no one pressuring me to write a blog or a book at all, so how silly.

Productivity has been a little devil on my shoulder, whispering in my ear for as long as I can remember. Or rather, it's the lack of productivity that causes the whispers (which is both a blessing and a curse, I suppose). When I noticed this feeling creeping in, I thought, *I'm not gonna be a prisoner to the blog I'm creating as a platform to release the book I'm writing by taking focus away from finishing the book itself!*

I'm not sure this exactly ties into the quote above because the person's approval I'm caring about here is a ghost in my own subconscious, not a physical being. But perhaps those ghostly little devils on our shoulders are the ones causing us to fill our bowl until it spills, to sharpen our knives until they're blunt, to chase whatever makes our hearts clench.

Anyway, it led me to question what other areas of my life where I'm a prisoner to my own expectations. Can you think of any in yours?

WHERE'S THE OFF SWITCH?

The Master said,
"It is not easy to find a man who can study for three years
without thinking about earning a salary."
—Analects of Confucius - Book 8, Chapter 12

Losing sleep over your job is so annoying, but flipping the mind's OFF switch to separate work and life has always been a challenge, especially since it takes up such a big chunk of time. I was expanding upon the notion of being a "prisoner" in certain capacities with a fellow philosopher (as voiced in the previous post), and careers were one of those "prisons" discussed.

I've romanticized the notion of casting away all material and monetary attachments and moving to an ashram in some far-off land to live unemployed, but I've also wondered if doing so would just be an escape. Sure, maybe there's freedom in becoming a monk—meditating your days away on the top of a mountain somewhere, living off the bare minimum and whatnot—but would I be doing it in the pursuit of enlightenment and happiness, or would I be doing it to avoid the frustrations and challenges that come with a "normal" life down here on earth?

There's plenty of growth and healing to be had in the face of tests in office politics or financial pursuits, as non-new age spiritual as those things might sound. I've worked through many triggers that have arisen in working a sales job over the last few years, including dealing with rejection, discomfort with public speaking, navigating the professional social landscape, and breaking through self-imposed financial limitations. Would those have come up while sitting in Lotus pose up on the hill? Certainly not in the same capacity as they did down here.

I think the answer (for me at least) is to find some kind of balance in it all, by getting in the float tank every Friday night to process the week, by journaling about life to hash out my thoughts. And then, of course, by putting imaginary pressure on myself to complete a book and blog on top of it all because, at the end of the day, I'm a workaholic and somehow find satisfaction in the imbalance. Please excuse my contradiction while I burn the candle at both ends.

NEITZSCHE FOR MORONS

The veil of falsehood shall be torn down from within you,
and Truth shall come to dwell in the mind.
Peace and happiness shall fill your mind deep within,
if you act according to truth and self-discipline.
—Siri Guru Granth - Ang 591

Thought of the day: In order to find the truth, don't we first have to sort through all the untruths?

This idea came up while reading *Beyond Good And Evil* for the first time. Boy, I've found reading Nietzsche is like doing a jigsaw puzzle flipped over. I recognize there are pieces, I recognize they fit together in some capacity, but I look to the box in hopes that my confidence of having assembled puzzles before might return, but to no avail. He seems to be stringing together individual words that my primitive brain can recognize, but their meaning in such a particular order doesn't compute.

Here's the middle of a sentence I'm struggling to understand as much as the beginning and ending, which are equally troublesome:

"…and our fundamental tendency is to assert that the falsest judgments (to which synthetic judgments a priori belong) are the most indispensable to us, that without granting as true the fictions of logic, without measuring reality against the purely invented world of the unconditional and self-identical, without a continual falsification of the world by means of numbers, mankind could not live..."

I once considered myself sharp, but after flailing to grasp this smoke of words, I now consider myself a degree duller.

Here's my primitive brain's understanding:

"...and our tendency to assume things incorrectly (because these assumptions exist in our mind independent of actual experience) is important to us, because without assuming these illogical things to be true, without looking through the lens of our unconscious beliefs, without lying to ourselves using calculated justifications, mankind couldn't live..."

How'd I do?

(Keep an eye out for my upcoming translation of this translation, called *Nietzsche For Morons*.)

Anyway, good luck sorting through those untruths today, so you can be peaceful and happy instead of just live.

Truthfully yours,

TDH

SMOOTH RIDER

*Know the Self as lord of the chariot,
the body as the chariot itself,
the discriminating intellect as charioteer,
and the mind as reins.
[...]
With a discriminating intellect as charioteer
and a trained mind as reins,
they attain the supreme goal of life
to be united with the Lord of Love.*
—Katha Upanishad - Third Part, Verses 3-9

I've been feeling angry and irritated quite often lately. Part of it could be bullshit at work, part of it could be the nonsense life throws at us, part of it could be things piling up as I burn the candle at both ends, but mostly it just seems to be, well, there, lurking at the core.

Myofascia is a web-like membrane that separates and contains every muscle of the body. Myofascial release is a manual therapy that can relieve chronic tension created by this connective tissue. I've found good results when it comes to emotional trauma release while receiving treatment from a practitioner. For me, it serves as a meditation in listening to whatever memories arise as tensions in different parts of the body are worked out.

The more I peel back layers of the onion in the process of healing, though, the more this anger seems to come bubbling up, like lava through a thinning crust of earth. But after 90 minutes of work on the same pec minor (the one over the heart), I was able to dust off a chain of memories of feeling neglected or unimportant as a child. Internalized anger at others became a protective mechanism during spells of vulnerability.

"It can't be me," said the frightened ego, "so it must be them!"

Shedding light on this stored reaction allowed me to let go of a childish (i.e., youthfully ignorant) need to control my surroundings that way.

So what if I was unimportant in the eyes of another, I thought as the physical and emotional tension dissolved. *There's nothing I can do about it now!*

All this to say that sometimes a wheel of the chariot is bent out of shape, and focusing on fixing that first can allow the charioteer to run a smoother ride.

Now, while this metaphor is cute to read, I believe that until you revisit the original memory and release the tension it caused in your body, mantras and meditations can be useless in creating lasting change on a subconscious level. So take hold of the reins and steer your chariot down those challenging paths. Or, perhaps, let them go.

AREN'T I THOUGH?

*With my own eyes,
I have seen those known as kings and lords reduced to dust.
O' Nanak, when one departs from the world,
all one's false attachments are broken.*
—Siri Guru Granth - Ang 16

I've been going back and forth with someone on the "I am not the body" philosophy, popular in yogic practices and, I believe, traced back to the Vedic traditions.

The belief is that "you" are eternal and, therefore, not attached to this material form. Of course, this requires a belief in the immortal soul, but I like to keep a grip on the fact that our life here and now is all we know for sure.

Maybe this is just a temporary meat vehicle, but I'll never truly be able to accept that we are not the body because we are so inevitably tied to the body. We are an accumulation of all the physical and psychological stimuli that have happened to us since birth. If a baby is mistreated in infancy, the body remembers what the conscious mind won't, and so your being becomes a sum of the subconscious reactions and stories shaped by traumas and experiences, even the ones before you remember. These can remain stored in the body as physical tensions, chronic pains, and poor postures that influence who we are. All of these shape the personality that is "you."

There are various means to heal these things (like meditation, acupuncture, therapy, psychedelics) or make them worse (like drugs, alcohol, or self-inflicted wounds), but they are both means of influencing or manipulating the body.

In the end, what is "you" if not the personality created by every experience you've ever had? Some cookie-cutter "soul" that comes from a spiritual dough to which it returns after death? I suppose that plays into the "all are one" and "from the source" ideas, but that view detracts from any meaning in the individual experience in the here and now.

I think my view boils down to not knowing what, if anything, comes after this life, and so I'm more concerned with making the here and now fulfilling. That starts with keeping the body as healthy as possible because it's directly tied to the mind, and, therefore, if such a thing exists, the soul. Any kind of healing we can perform during the "you" experience now can only carry over to a spiritual or karmic afterlife, if anything like that truly does exist.

BE THE GARDNER

*There is no guarantee that you will survive,
even past this very day!
The time has come for you to develop
perseverance in your practice.*
—The Tibetan Book of the Dead - Chapter 1

I've been meditating to this soundtrack of wind chimes, Tibetan bowls, and the like. When I can empty my mind and focus on the sounds, I call that "Reality." When the mind drifts into thoughts of the past, speculation of the future, or nonsensical daydreams, I label that "Illusion." When I catch myself drifting into Illusion, I refocus and center myself in Reality. Taking this a step further, anytime a thought seems productive or conducive to my well-being, I observe it and let it go. But anytime a thought seems counterproductive, negative, or nonsensical, I "pluck" it from the garden like a weed (to use an unoriginal metaphor).

I spend a lot of time reading various sources of ancient wisdom—in search of how to achieve happiness or prosperity, I suppose—but while that may be good for planting the occasional flower, I've realized that no one can weed the garden but the gardener themself. This concept is nothing new, of course (it's been around for more than a couple of thousand years), but I think it hit me in a new way this morning when this question arose out of the abyss: "How can you bend Illusion to serve your Reality?"

Something about that line, paired with reading the above quote just before laying down for meditation, seemed noteworthy.

NOTES FROM FLOATS

The good renounce attachment for everything.
The virtuous do not prattle with a yearning for pleasures.
The wise show no elation or depression
when touched by happiness or sorrow.
—The Dhammapada - Chapter 6, Verse 83

"It's not the person that stirs your emotions, but rather their actions that mirror the actions of whoever caused the original trauma." This was an idea that came to mind as I climbed out of the float tank last night. It felt significant enough to write down, but I sat in the lounge for a while afterward, trying to figure out why.

I think it has something to do with taking back the power someone has over you. If you believe someone else is causing you to feel a certain way, that person's actions are out of your control, so the power lies with them. But if you realize the trauma within you is causing you to react a certain way, then you can address the trauma, and the power to curb your reaction lies with you.

The thought came after seemingly random anger bubbled up inside me toward the end of my float regarding how certain friendships fade over time. Of course, this just happens, as life does, and it's the attachment to these fading relationships that stirs emotions, but I realized I was holding on to feelings of anger toward the individuals themselves when what was actually causing my emotions was the reminder of an original abandonment trauma in the past.

Yet another gem from the #NotesFromFloats series.

Now it's time to let that sh*t go...

THIRTY YEARS IN THREE HOURS

Hatreds never cease through hatred in this world;
through love alone they cease.
This is an eternal law.
—*The Dhammapada - Chapter 1, Verse 5*

The other night, I spent three hours in the float tank. It might sound like a while, but I became so immersed in processing past traumas that it turned into a truly timeless experience.

One thing that surfaced was some anger I've been holding onto since high school. I was surprised to see this incident pop up, as I thought I'd moved through it already. However, this was a slightly different angle of the same experience, showing how long even nuanced baggage can linger in your body if you never address it.

I let my body do as it would in this relaxed state as I faced the same recurring emotions. Often, this includes unwinding in weird positions, certain muscle contractions, or even an uncontrolled (almost seizure-like) shaking of the head at times. It's really quite strange to observe, and not as easily achieved in meditations where gravity and other stimuli are involved. It's like the negative tensions are being squeezed out, much like wringing out a towel soaked in water.

I'm continually surprised by how many layers of the onion there are to peel away. Countless times I've addressed major incidents in my life and thought, *There. I'm all healed now!* But nope. More subtle layers still exist as I dig further and further. I guess it makes sense since there are thirty-plus years of life to dig through, but most of them seem to stem from adolescence and the earlier, more formative years.

After being wrung out, something that came to mind was how the other person involved was a "pawn" of God (for lack of a better term), steering me down a path that has influenced the life I live today. I held onto hatred for this person for so long, but now I could see that he was really a brother of mine, shaping me into the man I am now. Without his actions, who knows what path my life could have taken. It might have been something completely different, less desirable, not the same as it is now. In realizing this, the hatred I once had turned into love, and the tension disappeared.

NIRVANA

The Master said,
"The gentleman understands what is moral.
The small man understands what is profitable."
—*The Analects of Confucius* - Book 4, Chapter 16

I've had some wild experiences in meditation, but last night in the float tank was among the wildest. Ninety minutes in, I pierced through a new level of consciousness that I had yet to achieve. The term that came to mind was the title of a book I read years ago called *Breaking Open the Head*. While there, I wondered if this was what the Buddha meant by Nirvana (though it feels strange to claim I reached transcendence or enlightenment or anything of that nature). I got out feeling high on drugs and even needed to hang around the studio for twenty minutes before I felt good enough to drive. It was intense, to say the least.

One of the intentions I went into the float with was around money. I'm in sales, which is competitive by nature, and the chase for commissions is never-ending, so the pursuit of profit is always at the forefront of my mind. This job has been an uphill struggle for me, while I've seen others seemingly close bigger deals with ease. My work ethic, my abilities, and my relationships with prospects and clients are all up there with the best of my colleagues, so I decided to look inward, as I've noticed psychological barriers have been the issue attracting other things in life before.

I grew up around frugality, so this was naturally infused into my line of thinking. I believe it was this scarcity mentality that played a role in limiting my financial profitability. But along with (hopefully) breaking through this inherited self-fulfilling prophecy, I was also shown awareness of my unhealthy obsession with money, or this idea of a lack of money.

I'm not struggling; I can pay my bills and put aside savings, yet I've been holding onto this constant tension regarding money that I finally released. I'm talking about a major physical relief I'm still recovering from as I write this the next morning.

Will truckloads of money begin falling into my lap at this point? Perhaps not. But at least I can breathe easier and focus on the moral pursuits in life.

That said, the moment I become rich—monetarily, that is—I'll be sure to let you know.

PIZZA OR BUST

> *If a superior man abandon virtue,*
> *how can he fulfill the requirements of that name?*
> *The superior man does not,*
> *even for the space of a single meal,*
> *act contrary to virtue.*
> —Analects of Confucius - Book 4, Chapter 5

Sometimes, timing in life is just too perfect.

I was in the float tank last night, meditating on these recent posts about seeing others in yourself and yourself in others. Here are some of the insights that came through:

~ I have been darkness, and now I am light. Be the light for those around me.

~ Recognize the inner child within everyone else as if it were me.

~ No longer seek others to fulfill my needs; instead, be the one others seek.

~ Be open and accepting to anyone who comes my way.

The moment I walked out of the studio with that meditative high, a man approached me, asking for food. He mentioned that he had been trying to turn over a new leaf, attempting to make an honest living, but had been having trouble landing steady work.

Often, when people ask for money, I don't give because I assume it's going to drugs or alcohol. But this man asked for food, and I could see the sobriety in his eyes. Plus, we were standing next to a pizza shop that sold slices with a glowing OPEN sign. There was nothing else I could do.

I bought a couple of slices and sat down with him while he ate, listening to his story: a former cocaine dealer with theft and felony charges on his record, but he acknowledged that he was young and foolish then.

He seemed sincere, even saving a slice for the friend who was letting him stay at his house. I pointed him toward a place I saw was hiring recently and he thanked me. Before we parted ways, he said, "I knew God was gonna send someone my way this evening."

Had I abandoned virtue, even for the space of a single meal, I would not have experienced the satisfaction that statement brought me.

I have been darkness, and now I am light.

Be the one others seek.

GETTING HUMBLED

Submit to God and you will have peace.
Then things will go well for you.
—Job 22:21

I've found that when your ego becomes inflated the most is when God humbles you the hardest. In this case, my head got so big that I threw my back out. Being primarily bedridden for more than a week gives you time to reflect on that sort of thing. It also gives you time to finish a draft of the manuscript you've been working on—in this case, a commentary on the book of Job.

One major takeaway from Job was how God will never fit into a box of theology. His plan is mysterious and will never align with platitudes about the wicked being punished and the righteous prospering.

Sometimes, you work so hard on the path God laid out for you that your emotions border on cocky. Then, for absolutely no karmic reason at all, you're slapped with a crippling setback. While it can be tempting to curse God and doubt His ways in those times, the book of Job guides us toward deepening our relationship with God instead.

That's why I've been making a point to express gratitude for the pain that has allowed me to focus more on things that can be done lying down—like reading, writing, and meditating, for example. Although it's painful to, well, move at all, I can still recognize things could be worse. At least I didn't lose my entire wealth, family, and health, like Job.

While the quote above may seem tempting to buy into, when read in the context of a bigger story, it's actually being delivered by a misguided 'comforter' who tries to fit God within his neat little theology. The truth is that sometimes God makes the righteous suffer for reasons beyond our understanding. In those times, though, we should hold onto the faith that there's a greater purpose building in the background.

#Namaste… in bed.

SMILE IN THE FACE OF _____.

Burn emotional attachment, and grind it into ink.
Transform your intelligence into the purest of paper.
Make the love of the Lord your pen,
and let your consciousness be the scribe.
—Siri Guru Granth - Ang 16

I don't know what this means exactly, but it sure sounds good, doesn't it?

That first line stuck out to me because that's exactly what I've been trying to do as of late.

Prime example: Yesterday I came down with some kind of flu that really knocked me on my ass. I mean debilitating migraines and hot-cold, hot-cold flashes all through the night. I could have gotten all woe-is-me, "someone bring me chicken noodle soup," but instead I embraced the reminder of vulnerability and tried to smile in the face of poor health.

That's what I've really been trying to do lately: Smile in the face of [anger, frustration, illness, or whatever it is]. To become the master of my emotions. To be a third-party observer as initial reactions fly by. To remain in the pursuit of stoicism, through sickness and health, till death do us part.

(Now really though: Could someone bring me some chicken noodle soup?)

BUDWEISER & CAT PISS

Those humble beings who are filled
with keen understanding and meditative contemplation,
even though they intermingle with others,
they remain distinct.
—Siri Guru Granth - Ang 23

I'll spare you the details of how this situation arose, but a friend of mine found himself in the middle of nowhere North Carolina, drinking a room-temperature Budweiser in a dingy, cat-piss apartment with no cat. Across from him on the couch was what he described as a lonely, angry white guy in his mid-twenties. The context of this meeting (that eerily resembles a scene from the Jeffrey Dahmer docuseries I watched recently) is irrelevant to what I plan to focus on here: his backstory.

The guy was born in Russia, where his biological parents gave him up to an orphanage. He was then adopted by an American couple who brought him over to the States. His adoptive father cheated on his adoptive mother and then got into a car accident that killed his mistress, so he killed himself. This inspired his wife to spiral down a rabbit hole of crack and eventually overdose. Oh, and somewhere in the midst of all this happening, this fella was molested by his adoptive sister.

Isn't that just a happy little way to start off life, where now you're left to work a minimum wage job with no friends and hate everything?

No one wants to hear a no-happy-ending, dead-end story, but they sure do put most of ours into perspective, don't they? That's the sole reason I share this with you: if you're feeling even the slightest bit of "woe is me" before reading this, like I was, watch it evaporate into thin air.

Remember to be filled with keen understanding and meditative contemplation and remain distinctly humble as you intermingle with others. And do yourself a favor: put your Budweiser on ice.

LETTING GO OF CONTROL

*If you look to others for fulfillment,
you will never truly be fulfilled.*
—*Tao Te Ching - Verse 44*

Three strange and buried memories surfaced during my last meditation:

1. I discovered childhood jealousy toward my cousin because my parents got divorced and his did not.
2. There was a group of kids on my elementary school bus that got picked up before me, so I always had to sit just outside the "good seats." This physical separation, along with a perceived emotional separation between kids whose parents hadn't gotten divorced and me, seemed to create an "outcast" barrier in my mind.
3. I used to play with the daughter of my mother's friend whenever my mother went over to visit. She was my age and fun and pretty and made me feel a warmth I hadn't known. It was the puppiest of puppy dog loves before I knew what love was, and she made that feeling of being an outcast go away.

But one day my mother stopped visiting that friend, and I never saw that girl again. So the feeling of no longer being an outcast was taken away by the very person at the root of my feeling like an outcast in the first place. And that was when I developed a resentment toward feeling out of control.

I wished my parents had never split up, but that was out of my control.

I wished I could have kept seeing that girl, but that was out of my control.

I wished I didn't feel like an outcast, but that was out of my control too.

At least, that last one was the story my subconscious mind had been holding onto.

But here, I was able to shine conscious awareness on the notion that someone else can lessen the feeling of being an outcast and instead actually let go of feeling like an outcast. The difference is that the former is never under our control: you can't control the way you feel about someone else; you can't control the way someone else feels about you; you can't control whether or not you find love at all; and even if you find love, you can't control the fact that life can often interfere. But what is in your control is letting go of the attachment to things that are out of your control while trusting that God has everything under control for you.

THE KEY?

If you want to enter life, keep the commandments.
[...]
'Honor your father and mother,'
and
'Love your neighbor as yourself.'
—Matthew 19:17-19

Ram Dass once said, "If you think you're enlightened, spend a week with your family." What he meant, of course, is that the pursuit of enlightenment in isolation is one thing, but revisiting the root of early traumas and triggers is a different story. Going back to spend two weeks living at home recently was a good check-in to see where I'm at along the enlightenment journey. I'm certainly not there yet, but I am much closer than I've been in the past.

My first reaction to reading the Bible quote above was something like, "Well, that's easier for you to say, Jesus. Your father was an all-loving God and your mother was a virgin who seemed like a very nice lady! You never had to deal with any kind of physically abusive father or crack-addict mother. Who are you to be the authority on parent-child relationships?"

(For the record, my own parents were not physically abusive or crack addicts. I simply used extreme examples for anyone else struggling to relate to this topic.)

After thinking it through, I realized that regardless of whether or not you think your parents deserve to be honored, harboring negative feelings toward anyone is detrimental to your own well-being, especially your parents, who were supposed to love you the way you'd hoped for but instead bumped and bruised you in various ways. But if you can get over any hurdle to honoring them, big or small—recognizing they gave you life and made you who you are—then that might just be the key to your ultimate liberation.

This shift is also the biggest step toward loving your neighbor, and, therefore, being able to navigate the world without the kinds of negative reactions that plague us when dealing with people who trigger us.

It's not your job to change your parents but to be able to honor them for who they are.

It's not your job to change your neighbor but to be able to love them for who they are.

Because ultimately, these things help you to live a more peaceful life for yourself.

DROP IT LIKE IT'S HOT

The Master said,
"Rotten wood cannot be carved;
a wall of dung cannot be whitewashed.
[...]
It used to be that with people,
when I heard what they said
I trusted their conduct would match.
Now I listen to what they say and observe their conduct."
—Analects of Confucius - Book 5, Chapter 10

Friends, family, colleagues, strangers: all of these, at some time or another, will do something contrary to what they say. No one is perfect. I understand this, but I'm still triggered by what I've found. It boils down to failed expectations and my attachment to them.

I've been embracing this concept of non-attachment lately, and it's truly something to keep at the forefront of the mind. Anytime feelings of anger, sorrow, or anxiety bubble up, I meet them with a mantra of "non-attachment," and they immediately lessen their hold over me. From there, I can view the situation from an objective point of view and evaluate what's going on.

A one-time offense of doing contrary to what's said is merely something to be noted, but repeating patterns are what should be taken into consideration. Still, your emotions aren't to get involved. Instead, your perception of the other person will change. (It's more difficult when that other person has some kind of influence over your life, but the point is that getting emotional over the situation never helps anything.)

This may result in outgrowing people you once looked up to, accepting that, and moving on. It's the attachment of what that person was "supposed to be" to you that nags at your feelings, but ultimately, other people's words and actions are out of your control, and all you can do is keep your own word and hope to be a shining influence for others.

I wrote this in my journal after a recent experience of failed expectations:

Drop need. Drop desire. Drop expectations.

Embrace flow. Embrace neutrality. Embrace non-attachment.

This mindset has helped mitigate the emotional response to things out of my control, and so I pass it along to you to do with it as you will.

G.I. JOE

Do not envy the violent or choose any of their ways.
—*Proverbs 3:31*

I've been spending time with an ex-military friend I met earlier this year at the archery range. We'll call him Joe.

His stories never cease to amaze me with how vastly different our lives have been. He seems to have been surrounded by violence from youth until now. Me? Not so much.

He's been in countless brawls; I have not.

He's seen terrible savagery at war and at home; I have not.

He's killed people; I have not.

Part of this may be a product of the environment we grew up in, specifically our high school systems, separated by decades of "progress"—the word some might use, while I believe Joe chose the word "pussification."

You see, back in Joe's day, fistfights occurred in school on a daily basis. That was just the culture then, and you had to fight to survive. By the time I went to school (at least where I grew up), you only saw the occasional fistfight every year, if you were lucky. It's likely because the punishment for the offense was more severe by then. In Joe's day, it was practically a slap on the wrist; in mine, suspension and the police were involved.

I wonder why one of us is surrounded by violence while the other is not still today. Why, just the other day, Joe had a gun pulled on him outside a restaurant on his lunch break. I mostly eat lunch at home, so maybe that's part of the equation, but still, how can someone attract so much violence when I seem to be skating by in the peaceful parts of town?

Were we just born on different paths? Are we drawn there because events in our past sowed repeating stories in our subconscious mind, manifesting themselves in reality? Is he seeking out what I'm avoiding?

Sometimes I wonder how I would have fared in war or dealt with the violence Joe has been exposed to, but at the end of the day, I'm on my path, and I don't envy his. However, his stories are fascinating to hear. Tune in tomorrow for a prime example.

"ALWAYS TAKE BODY PARTS WITH YOU."

He who inflicts violence on those who are unarmed,
and offends those who are inoffensive,
will soon come upon one of these ten states:
Sharp pain, or disaster,
bodily injury, serious illness, or derangement of mind,
trouble from the government, or grave charges,
loss of relatives, or loss of wealth,
or houses destroyed by ravaging fire;
upon dissolution of the body that ignorant man is born in hell.
—The Dhammapada - Chapter 10, Verses 137-140

Have you ever ripped someone's ear off?

Yeah, me neither. But Joe has (my ex-military friend mentioned in the prior post). Then he smashed the guy's leg with a cinder block to finish off the fight.

Was this in war, you ask? Was this a means of survival?

Well, more like a dispute over a wave while surfing at the beach.

To be fair, the other guy started it; Joe just finished it. (At least that's how Joe tells the story.)

This whole event came to the surface when Joe asked what I did last weekend. When I told him I'd recently bought a surfboard, he said, "Oh, Jesus. You're done for." When I expressed my conviction that sharks don't like the way I taste, he said, "It's not the sharks you have to look out for. It's the surfers. They can be real assholes."

Only having met nice surfers so far, I asked him to expand upon what he meant. And so trickled into my own ear the tale of how he accidentally bumped into another wave rider who had a bit of a temper when it came to surfing etiquette.

Joe was confronted by this long-haired troublemaker back on the beach and tackled him into the sand. On break from his military duties and trained in martial arts, Joe had the good wits to grab hold of this fellow's auditory appendage and bring him to the ground with him.

"He left the beach without an ear that day," said Joe, not expanding much more on the fight, other than the grand finale of cinder block smashing. Then he said, "I'll give you a piece of advice when it comes to fighting. Always take body parts with you."

Then, like it was nothing, he transitioned into what a good workout surfing can be. Imagine being so numb to violence that a story about ripping another guy's ear off just sort of fades into the background as you discuss the cardiovascular benefits of paddling through tides.

I think what Buddha's trying to say here is, don't pick a fight with someone unless you know who you're fighting, lest some bodily injury soon come upon thee. Or, perhaps, don't pick a fight at all.

TRUE BRAVERY

One who eradicates his own evil is a brave warrior[...].
Man is bound by the chains of his own
egotism, selfishness, and conceit.
The spiritually blind place the blame on others.
—Siri Guru Granth - Ang 258

I've heard it called brave to talk about emotions. Well, my ex-military friend Joe once told me about a Special Forces unit made up of the most badass of badasses. They jump from planes and parachute deep behind enemy lines alone to carry out the most dangerous missions. No food, no water, no form of communication—just whatever they can carry on their backs as they jump out of a plane.

The only reassurance they get from their commanding officer is something like, "Don't come back until the mission's complete. Oh, and good luck finding your own way home." Apparently, rescue for these brave souls isn't an option, considering the restrictive circumstances they're operating under.

Even if they complete their mission and make it home, chances are another mission will be waiting for them upon arrival. It's likely that one day, they won't make it home at all, and their bones will remain somewhere behind enemy lines forever. And yet, they still jump. Now *that's* brave.

Anytime I feel resistance toward being emotionally vulnerable, toward dealing with a situation I don't want to, toward digging into a past memory I'd prefer to avoid, I remind myself what true bravery looks like, and it puts my own situation in perspective.

STRANGER STRANGLER

*Do not take revenge, my dear friends,
but leave room for God's wrath, for it is written:
"It is Mine to avenge; I will repay," says the Lord.*
—Romans 12:19

I plan to share this story in full in another book, but when I was in high school, I was tackled to the ground and choked by a grown man twice my size for "touching his wife" (essentially tapping her on the shoulder in the grocery store). I've processed this memory from a few different angles already—the fear of having my life threatened, the inability to breathe as I began to black out, the violation of someone forcing themselves upon me—but apparently, I had one more angle to process: forgiveness.

This was probably the most difficult hurdle in my trauma-processing journey so far. I really had to wrestle my ego into submission as it struggled to hold onto the notion that "this man doesn't *deserve* forgiveness!" While that might be true, the idea expressed in the quote above popped into mind and helped me realize that holding onto murderous thoughts of revenge wasn't doing me any favors.

I've experienced something akin to convulsions when processing trauma before (which I've described as something like wringing out a towel full of anger, hatred, or fear), but what I experienced in letting this go was an intensity to the degree I felt a blood vessel might burst in my eye.

Being violated by a man twice their size is something no child should have to go through, but I am a believer that everything happens for a reason, and the experience of overcoming this hurdle in forgiveness was—dare I say—almost worth having the experience itself.

Replacing my hatred with compassionate wonder for what happened to this man that he'd go as far as to strangle a boy felt like walking in Christ-like shoes. I found myself sympathizing with someone who was, perhaps, molested as a child, and who felt tapping his wife on the shoulder was a violation of boundaries, and I even envisioned myself embracing this person with the hug they've probably needed for a very long time.

Processing this experience was for my own benefit, I suppose, but I hope sharing this story has the power to inspire someone else to work through their own healing journey.

CHAOS OR FATE?

*We may throw the dice,
but the Lord determines how they fall.*
—*Proverbs 16:33*

A friend of mine hand-delivered a copy of my book, *Genesis: Biblical Commentary Through Dialogue*, to Jordan Peterson. (Whether it ends up in some dusty pile of fan mail or is actually thumbed through, I may never know, but it sounds good, doesn't it?) After she told me this, I reflected on all the events that led up to such a thing.

Jordan was my inspiration for opening the Bible in the first place, so without his lectures, I never would have written a book on Genesis at all. Without tuning into Joe Rogan's podcast, I never would have joined the float tank studio where I met this friend. Without this friend experiencing some mysterious health concerns, she never would have joined the float studio either. And without her nephew graduating from Ralston College, where Jordan is Chancellor, she never would have had the opportunity to cross his path.

There alone are five lives woven together that led up to this event. And then, of course, are all the lives and events that led each of us to where we were for it all to happen. And on, and on, and on, traced back until the beginning of time.

Was it fate? Random chaos? God's plan?

It's just weird to think about who could have turned left instead of right at any point in time and mucked up the whole thing unfolding. The intertwining of all people and things is such a curious thing to puzzle over.

I don't know where I'm going with this. I have no humor to interject or profound wisdom to impart; just the simple observation that life is strange, and maybe the reminder that, as much as we like to think we're in control of certain aspects of our lives, so much more goes into how things play out for us.

PYRAMID OF PRIORITIZATION

But seek first the kingdom of God and his righteousness, and all these things will be provided for you.
—Matthew 6:33

When distributing time and energy across various aspects of life, you could do worse than the following structure of prioritization.

Imagine a pyramid with different layers—the bottom and largest layer representing where you should focus the most attention, moving upwards toward areas of decreasing priority—the order is as follows:

Community

Family/Friends

Children

Partner

Self

God

Here's why:

God - Whether or not you believe in a pervading spirit that inspired holy scripture and controls events, expressing gratitude toward something higher, seeking guidance through meditation, or manifesting desires through prayer by invoking the law of attraction are powerful tools. They can help you navigate the moral landscape of life and fulfill your destiny.

<u>Self</u> - Without taking care of yourself—in mental, physical, and spiritual health—you can't possibly be the best partner, parent, friend, or member of your community you need to be.

<u>Partner</u> - If you choose to have a family, the foundational layer the children stand on is that of the relationship between their parents. While there may be examples where this ordering can be debated, in an ideal world, you've built such a foundation with the first two layers that you've made the right choice of spouse before having children.

<u>Children</u> - The obligation tied to this layer of the pyramid doesn't need spelling out, but you can only provide the best for your offspring after putting forth the effort to establish the previous layers.

<u>Family/Friends</u> - Of importance, of course, but the nuclear family should come before others, as the main responsibility is raising children who will one day venture off into the world to either contribute to the production or destruction of society.

<u>Community</u> - As beneficial as social organizations can be, they shouldn't take priority over everything that precedes them here. And even further from your attention should be things happening outside your immediate purview.

DHARMA BUMS

It is better to do one's own dharma, even though imperfectly, than to do another's dharma, even though perfectly.
—The Bhagavad Gita - Chapter 18, Verse 47

I have this inner guiding voice of sorts—what the Socratic Greeks might have called a "daemon," I suppose. It began as gut feelings or intuitions, but somewhere along my journey, I realized I could dialogue with it.

One night, this voice woke me up with an idea, as it has done many times over the years. After I wrote it down, I got the inkling to ask this voice what it was. I closed my eyes and drifted back to the half-conscious state in which the communications began, and the conversation went something like this:

"What are you?"

"I am you, from the future."

"Then how am I manifesting the signs I ask for in the outer world?"

"You're not. I AM." (Capitalized because it came through in the Exodus 3:14 sense—"I AM WHO I AM"—the mysterious description of God's nature that cannot be declared in words or conceived of by human thought.)

"So I'm God..?"

"You are me—past, present, and future you, all bound by free will." (The second part seemed oxymoronic, but I didn't question it, while the first part reminded me of how Atman—a person's innermost soul—is also Brahman—the transcendent being/reality that pervades the universe—extended across time.)

"What else can you tell me?"

"Follow my will to become what you're supposed to be."

"Can I write about this?"

"That's your purpose, isn't it? Now go."

And so I went, and so I wrote.

Take from that what you will, but I imagine everyone has access to this voice if they listen carefully (as we're all manifestations of the same pervading being/reality). Though, I'd venture to guess many hear what's essentially a dial tone when they pick up the line or choose to ignore whatever comes through anyway.

Socrates went as far as to follow this voice to his death, though that appeared to be his destiny, and probably what made him immortal in the sense that his name lives on. I've been following mine for quite a while, reluctantly at times, but it seems to have led me down a good path so far. So, I suppose trusting that it will guide me toward "what I'm supposed to be" would make it a mistake to do otherwise.

So my advice to you is: listen up, dharma bums.

LIKE LIGHTNING

*As in nature
a single flash of lightning illumines everything,
so [...] do the impressions of some people.*
—The Brihadaranyaka Upanishad - Chapter 2, Section 3,
Verse 6

Last night was one of the most intense lightning storms I've ever witnessed, the kind of storm where the night was often lit up like day. At one point, it seemed there were more flashes of lightning in the sky than there were moments without.

For some strange reason, in the midst of all this, my friend's dad popped into my mind. I haven't seen him in years. I haven't talked to him in years. I haven't thought much about him in years. There was a point in adolescence when he was one of the more prominent father figures in my life. I spent a lot of time around him, growing up in my friend's house, and looked up to him as a role model. Unfortunately, due to circumstances, he had to move back to his home country, and I never saw him again.

This storm appeared to be a metaphorical reminder that some people, no matter how prevalent in your life at one time, can disappear in a flash, never to be seen again. I was too young to recognize the fleeting presence of people around me then, but the older I get, the more aware I become of how little time we have left with the people around us.

Recently, I attended a wedding and reunited with a group of people who were my best friends in college. I realized I haven't seen any of them in six or eight years—people I lived with, people I saw on a daily basis, people who are now closer to distant memories. Just like that rare kind of lightning storm, my remaining experiences with these college pals will be few and far between, if there are any left at all.

If you live a flight away from your friends and family, as I do, the number of times you visit even your closest kin is once or twice per year. The remaining opportunities to see them could be counted on your fingers and toes in some cases.

These facts are sobering notions when you weigh them in your mind. Like a passing storm, the opportunities will soon have gone by, leaving you only with the vague memories of what went down—a distant, echoing rumble in the background.

DEATH GRIP

We are men of but one breath
and know not the appointed time or moment
of our departure from this world.
—*Siri Guru Granth - Ang 660*

I often sit on my balcony and observe the birds that inhabit the lake. There's a flock of pigeons that flies around together, and sometimes, I meditate on their cooing and fluttering sounds. In the past, there was this one albino pigeon that stood out from the rest. I'll probably never know what happened to her, but one day, she disappeared, and I haven't seen her since.

I was meditating recently and a middle school crush of mine—whom I hadn't thought about much since then—popped into mind. I realized how her teasing me back then had planted a kind of minor insecurity that I'd apparently been harboring for all these years. After letting that go, I decided to look her up on social media and even considered reaching out after all this time to say hello.

Turns out she's dead now.

It was kind of jarring, really. I don't know why; she's been nothing but a foggy memory for the greater part of my conscious life. But discovering the death of someone who had influenced one of the stories I've been holding onto was sobering for whatever reason. I think it was a reminder that people who aren't even alive anymore can still have a grip over your life if you're not adamant about seeking out even the most minor of traumas.

I don't think there's much more to be said on the matter, but to sum this up with a parallel metaphor: just as the albino pigeon disappeared into the ether, so too has this young lady and her influence over my unconscious mind.

NOSTALGIA

*He who clings to nothing of the past, present, and future,
who has no attachment and holds on to nothing,
him do I call a holy man.*
—The Dhammapada - Chapter 26, Verse 421

About once a year, I have the chance to drive through the old neighborhood I grew up in, and it never fails to trigger a sense of nostalgia.

Back when pedal-powered transportation was your main ride, you could almost always zoom around long enough to find some other kid outside to play with. And if no one was outside, well, there were always a few houses you could barge into like you owned the place, announcing your unexpected arrival. Your friends' families were your families, and vice versa.

But the days of welcome familiarity are gone. Now it's like driving through a ghost town, with strangers inhabiting your old stomping grounds, odd owners illuminating rooms you once played in, eating from the refrigerators you once ate out of, swimming in the pools you once splashed in.

The memories of the past surface and drift by like smoke as you fail to reach out and grasp each of them one last time. The corner where your friend ran his lemonade stand, the crest of the hill the bus dropped you off on, the poison ivy path you'd cut through to save a longer walk around: all just a graveyard with various headstones labeled, "Here lies the memory of [X, Y, or Z]." You see the houses of once great friends and wonder what they're up to these days, realizing it's as easy to lose track of others as it is to lose track of time. This inevitable truth of life floats by like the river you once fished out of as children, the image of friends as foggy as the memories themselves. A few of them are already dead and gone, while a few more of them will disappear as time drifts by.

I don't know why I even drive through the old streets anymore; I could just as easily avoid stirring up these feelings of nostalgia. But instead, I let it run through me like a haunting spirit who's come back to collect his due, palm out with the expectation I'll cough up more emotions.

What is a trip down memory lane even good for, when all that's ahead is the unknown?

Maybe that's just it, though: a longing for comfort in the illuminated past while faced with the daunting darkness of the future.

Or perhaps it's just a necessary reminder that time consumes us all.

THE BUTTERFLY LADY

*One generation commends your works to another;
they tell of your mighty acts.
—Psalms 145:4*

During the thirty-ish years my grandmother spent teaching third grade, she was known as "The Butterfly Lady." Every summer, she would venture out into the fields around town and collect monarch butterfly eggs from the milkweed that shot up through the grass. She'd gather at least one egg for every student, and these eggs would hatch into hungry caterpillars kept under the safeguard of clear plastic cups in cardboard trays. These "pillars" had to be fed with leaves for a week or so before they'd climb to the top of their cup, hang to shed their skin, and form a chrysalis.

I was a fortunate witness to this phenomenon early in life, holding freshly sprouted butterflies from the time I could form sentences, watching them pump their wings until they were healthy enough to fly. Seeing this life cycle engraved some of my earliest memories. Of course, as a child, I only saw the birth, growth, and fluttering away parts of this cycle. It wasn't until later that I learned how the cycle ends.

As of late, the monarchs have been slowly disappearing. Humans have created a world where the coming generations have a daunting task to survive. A friend and I were talking the other day about whether we'd care to bring our own offspring into a world so fraught with danger and perils, as the pending apocalypse seems to be at nigh. But after further reflection, we figured the apocalypse has always been coming, always just around the corner. Your parents thought so, their parents thought so, and their parents thought so too. And yet, the generations keep on coming.

Hundreds of monarchs flew from the cups my grandmother hung in her classroom. The impending doom of declining numbers never gave her an excuse to give up trying. She kept up with this tradition until, as all life cycles do, hers came to an end. If any lesson can be gleaned from this story, I suppose it's one of optimistic persistence, where our own generation can aspire to be like her, raising one little metaphorical caterpillar at a time and hoping to see them flutter off into the world on their own.

Thank you for reading!

Do you have a minute to support the author with a review?

www.ingramcontent.com/pod-product-compliance
Lightning Source LLC
Chambersburg PA
CBHW071455040426
42444CB00008B/1343